THE PEANUT GENIUS

THE STORY OF GEORGE WASHINGTON CARVER FOR KIDS

JAMES SMITH

BOOKSTEM

Copyright © 2025 by James Smith

All rights reserved.

No part of this book may be reproduced in any form or by any electronic or mechanical means, including information storage and retrieval systems, without written permission from the author, except for the use of brief quotations in a book review.

CONTENTS

1. A HUMBLE BEGINNING — 5
   Born into slavery during the Civil War — 9
   Growing up on a farm in Missouri — 13
   His love for learning — 17
   Struggles to get an education — 21

2. THE POWER OF EDUCATION — 27
   Finding teachers and mentors who encouraged him — 31
   Attending College — 35
   Becoming the first Black student and later the first Black professor at Iowa State — 38

3. A SCIENTIST WITH A MISSION — 43
   Helping poor farmers improve their crops — 46
   Understanding the problem with soil depletion — 49
   Teaching crop rotation — 52

4. THE MANY USES OF PEANUTS — 57
   Discovering over 300 uses for peanuts, including paints, oils, and soaps — 60
   His work with sweet potatoes and other crops — 62
   Promoting self-sufficiency for farmers — 65

5. CARVER'S IMPACT BEYOND
   THE FARM   69
   Working with Booker T. Washington at
   Tuskegee   71
   Meeting famous people   74
   His efforts to improve racial relations
   through science   77

6. HIS LEGACY LIVES ON   81
   His simple life and belief in helping
   others   83
   The George Washington Carver
   National Monument   86
   How his work still impacts farming
   and science today   88

7. FUN FACTS ABOUT GEORGE
   WASHINGTON CARVER   93
   The peanut and sweet potato myths   95
   How he turned down great wealth to
   keep helping farmers   99
   His advice for young scientists and
   dreamers   102

   *Conclusion: What We Can Learn from
   Carver*   107
   Glossary   119
   Discussion Questions   125
   Simple science activities   131
   Careers in science and agriculture   139

1

A HUMBLE BEGINNING

George Washington Carver was born at a time when life was anything but easy. He entered the world during the Civil War, when the United States was divided, and people like him—Black Americans—were often treated unfairly. He wasn't born in a hospital or in a big house. Instead, he came into the world on a small farm in Diamond, Missouri, owned by Moses and Susan Carver, a white couple who had enslaved his parents.

Before George was even old enough to walk, the war ended, and slavery was abolished. That meant he and his family were no longer owned by anyone. But freedom didn't mean an easy life. His parents had disappeared—his mother was kidnapped, likely taken away and never found—and George and his brother, James, were left to be raised by the Carvers. Even though he was no longer a slave, being a free Black child in the 1860s meant there were still many challenges ahead.

From the very start, George was different. While other kids his age spent their days playing or helping with chores, George was fascinated by the world around him. He wanted to understand everything—how plants grew, why the soil smelled different after it rained, and what made flowers bloom in different colors. He didn't just look at nature; he studied it.

The Carvers, though not his real family, allowed him to explore. They taught him basic reading and writing at home since there weren't many schools that would accept Black students. But learning at home wasn't enough for George. He wanted more.

That's when he heard about a school for Black children a few miles away. It wasn't a fancy school with big classrooms or lots of books. It was a small, one-room schoolhouse with just a few supplies. That didn't matter to George. He had waited long enough to sit in a real classroom, and nothing was going to stop him.

But there was one big problem. The school wasn't close. It was miles away, too far to walk back and forth every day. Most kids would have given up. George didn't. Instead, he packed up what little he had and set out on his own, determined to get an education.

That was just the beginning.

George traveled from town to town, always looking for new places to learn. He worked as a farmhand, did chores in exchange for meals, and even slept outdoors when he had no other choice. Some towns turned him away because they didn't allow Black students in their schools. That didn't stop him. He just kept moving forward, finding new teachers, new books, and new ways to grow his knowledge.

One of the first schools he attended was in Neosho, Missouri. When he arrived, he had nowhere to stay. That's when he met Mariah and Andrew Watkins, an African American couple who let him live with them in exchange for doing chores. He spent his days learning in school and his evenings working for the Watkins family, studying by candlelight when the chores were done.

Even though he had finally made it into a classroom, he quickly realized that he already knew more than most of the students. He had spent years teaching himself, reading everything he could get his hands on, and paying attention to the world around him.

But he wasn't done yet. He wanted more than just a basic education. He wanted to go to college.

That was almost unheard of for a Black student at the time. Few colleges accepted African American students, and even when they did, it was rare. George applied anyway. He was accepted into Highland University in Kansas—only to be turned away once they realized he was Black.

Most people would have been heartbroken. George just kept going.

He traveled again, working wherever he could to support himself, until he found a school that would accept him. Simpson College in Indianola, Iowa, took him in. At first, he studied art—he was talented at drawing and painting, especially plants and flowers. But one of his professors noticed something special about him. He didn't just paint plants; he understood them.

That's when he was encouraged to study agriculture—the science of farming.

That decision changed everything.

George transferred to Iowa State Agricultural College (now Iowa State University), where he became not just a student, but eventually a teacher and researcher. He was the first Black student at the college and later became its first Black professor. He spent his time studying soil, crops, and ways to help farmers grow better food. He didn't want to be rich or famous. He wanted to help people—especially poor farmers—find better ways to work the land.

George Washington Carver wasn't just smart. He was determined. He knew that knowledge was the key to making life better, and he never let anything—not poverty, not racism, not rejection—stop him from learning.

Born into slavery during the Civil War

George Washington Carver entered the world in a time of chaos. The United States was in the middle of the Civil War, a brutal fight that had torn the country apart. On one side were the Union states, which wanted to end slavery. On the other were the Confederate states, which fought to keep it. While armies clashed on battlefields across the country, life carried on in small towns and farms, including the one where George was born.

He took his first breath in Diamond, Missouri, sometime around 1864. No one wrote down the exact date, and there were no birth certificates for enslaved children. George later guessed that he was born in the final year of the war, but there was no way to be sure. What is certain is that his life began with hardship.

George and his family belonged to Moses and Susan Carver, a white couple who owned a small farm. Like many enslaved people, his parents had no freedom. They couldn't leave. They couldn't choose their own jobs. They worked from sunrise to sunset, planting crops, taking care of animals, and doing whatever their owners told them to do. Their future wasn't their own—it belonged to someone else.

Then everything changed.

In 1865, the Civil War ended, and slavery was abolished. That should have meant a new beginning, but for George, it came with loss. His mother, Mary, disappeared. Some say she was kidnapped by raiders who captured freed Black people and sold them back into slavery in the South. Others believe she was taken in the middle of the night and never seen again. No one really knows what happened to her. George was still just a baby when she vanished, leaving him and his brother, James, alone.

The Carvers, now no longer their owners but the only family they had left, raised the two boys. Life on the farm wasn't easy. They didn't have money, and work had to be done every day just to survive. George was small and not as strong as his brother, so he was given lighter chores. Instead of plowing fields or chopping wood, he helped around the house, tended to the garden, and spent time exploring the land around him. That's where his love of nature really began.

There was something about the way plants grew that fascinated him. While other children might see a flower and walk right past it, George stopped to study it. He wanted to know why certain plants flourished while others wilted. He noticed how different soils affected growth and how tiny insects played a role in pollination. These weren't things most kids thought about, but George wasn't like most kids.

Books were hard to come by on the Carver farm, but that didn't stop him from learning. Susan Carver taught him to read and write, and he practiced whenever he could. He used sticks to trace letters in the dirt and borrowed books whenever someone would lend him one. He read everything he could find, even though there weren't many books available to him.

But reading wasn't enough. He wanted to learn from people who knew more than he did. He wanted to go to school. That wasn't simple for Black children in Missouri. Schools for African Americans were rare, and even when they existed, they weren't close by. The nearest school was miles away. That didn't stop George.

One morning, he packed what little he had and set off on foot, determined to learn. It didn't matter that he had no money. It didn't matter that he had no place to stay. What mattered was that education was out there, and he was going to find it.

That journey, started on a dirt road in Missouri, would take him across many towns and many schools. Some places welcomed him. Others turned him away. He worked for food and shelter, taking any small job he could find, just so he could sit in a classroom.

Those early years shaped him. They taught him that knowledge was something no one could take away. It didn't matter that he had been born into slavery. It didn't matter that the world didn't make things easy for him. What mattered was that he was willing to fight for his future.

Growing up on a farm in Missouri

Every morning, as the first streaks of sunlight stretched across the sky, George Washington Carver was already awake. Life on the Carver farm didn't allow for sleeping in. There were chores to do, animals to tend, and meals to prepare. But George's mornings looked a little different from his brother James's. While James was expected to do the heavier farm work—plowing fields, chopping wood, and hauling water—George had smaller tasks, ones that didn't require as much strength.

He didn't mind.

There was something about the quiet moments before the farm bustled with activity that he loved. The dew clung to the grass, the air smelled fresh, and the world felt wide open. While others focused on work that kept the farm running, George paid attention to things most people overlooked. He noticed the way certain plants curled their leaves before a rainstorm. He studied how insects moved from flower to flower, carrying pollen. He ran his fingers through the soil, feeling the difference between dry, cracked earth and rich, healthy dirt.

Curiosity pulled him toward the land, and he let it.

The Carver farm wasn't large, but it had everything a working farm needed. There were fields for growing crops, a vegetable garden, and animals that provided milk, eggs, and meat. The Carvers weren't wealthy. They didn't own vast acres of land or have hired workers. Instead, they relied on hard work to keep food on the table.

George helped where he could. He learned to gather eggs from the chickens, careful not to startle them. He pulled weeds from the garden, noticing which ones came back quickly and which ones struggled to survive. When Susan Carver showed him how to make simple herbal remedies from plants, he listened closely, remembering every detail. He was fascinated by the idea that something growing in the dirt could be used to heal a cut or cure a stomachache.

His fascination didn't stop there.

Whenever he finished his chores, he slipped away to explore the woods and fields surrounding the farm. He carried a small sack with him, stuffing it with interesting leaves, rocks, and anything else that caught his eye. While other children might have spent their free time playing games, George spent his collecting and studying. He wanted to understand the world around him, not just accept it as it was.

But curiosity wasn't always welcomed.

James, who spent his days doing the backbreaking work of farming, didn't understand why George got to spend so much time with books and plants. To him, hard work meant sweating in the sun and pushing through exhaustion. George, always looking for answers in nature, seemed to be avoiding real work. Their differences created tension, and while they were brothers, they weren't always close.

Moses and Susan Carver had their own expectations. They had taken George in after slavery ended, raising him as best they could. But they didn't fully understand his deep need to learn. They saw his interest in nature as strange. Useful, maybe, but not something that could put food on the table. Farming was about survival, not curiosity.

But George saw something different.

He noticed how the same fields, planted year after year, produced smaller and weaker crops. He saw how the land became dry and lifeless when people didn't take care of it properly. To him, farming wasn't just about planting seeds and hoping for the best. It was about understanding the land, listening to it, and finding ways to make it healthier.

The Carvers didn't discourage him, but they didn't encourage him either. They gave him the freedom to learn in his own way but didn't see much use in it. If he wanted to spend his time collecting plants and studying the soil, that was his choice. But they weren't going to stop running their farm the way they always had.

That was why school became so important to George.

The Carver farm had given him a foundation. It had shown him the value of hard work, the cycles of nature, and the importance of taking care of the land. But he wanted more. He wanted to know why some plants thrived and others didn't. He wanted to understand how soil worked, not just accept that some fields were fertile while others weren't.

And he knew he wasn't going to find those answers on the farm.

That knowledge existed somewhere else, in books, in schools, in places where people dedicated their lives to studying the things he loved. Getting there wouldn't be easy, but George had already learned one thing that would guide him for the rest of his life: when something matters, you don't give up.

His love for learning

Every step George took outside felt like stepping into a classroom. But unlike a schoolhouse, his classroom had no walls, no blackboards, and no desks. Instead, it was filled with trees that whispered in the wind, flowers that stretched toward the sun, and soil that crumbled between his fingertips. Nature was his teacher, and he was always ready to learn.

Plants fascinated him in a way that nothing else did. He could spend hours studying the different shades of green in the leaves of an oak tree or tracing the winding paths of vines as they climbed up fence posts. He watched bees dip into flowers, their legs dusted with golden pollen, and wondered what made them choose one bloom over another. If a plant looked sick, he didn't just walk past it—he knelt beside it, inspecting its leaves, searching for clues. Was it too dry? Was the soil too thin? Was something eating away at it?

On the Carver farm, most people saw plants as food or crops, something that needed to grow in order to survive. But George saw them as living puzzles.

He wanted answers to questions no one else seemed to be asking. Why did certain flowers bloom at different times of the year? Why did the roots of some plants grow deep while others spread wide across the surface? And most importantly, why did some crops flourish while others failed?

The answers weren't always obvious, but that was what made learning exciting.

Without many books to turn to, George relied on his own experiments. He would dig up soil from different spots around the farm, comparing its color and texture. Some dirt was dark and rich, full of life. Other patches were pale and dry, crumbling at the slightest touch. He wanted to know why.

He began testing different ways to care for plants, even before he knew the science behind it. He added crushed eggshells to the soil and noticed that some plants grew stronger. He moved sickly plants to different spots in the garden and watched as some of them recovered. He paid attention to things most people overlooked—small changes in color, the way leaves drooped when they needed water, how worms wriggled through the soil, making it looser and easier for roots to grow.

None of this felt like work. It felt like uncovering secrets hidden beneath the earth.

Books became just as important to him as the soil under his feet. The problem was, there weren't many around. He borrowed whatever he could, sometimes reading the same book over and over, memorizing details about plants and farming. He would sit under a tree or beside the garden, flipping through pages, hungry for knowledge.

When he heard about a school for Black children in Neosho, Missouri, he knew he had to go. It didn't matter that it was miles away from the Carver farm. It didn't matter that he had no money, no place to stay, and no plan. He just knew that if there were books and teachers, it was where he needed to be.

Traveling alone wasn't safe, but staying put wasn't an option. He packed what little he had and walked the dusty roads to Neosho, driven by nothing more than his love for learning.

When he finally reached the school, he realized something—learning in a classroom was different from learning in the fields. In nature, there were no limits. He could study as long as he wanted, ask as many questions as he pleased. But in school, he had to follow rules, wait his turn, and listen to lessons that didn't always move as fast as his thoughts.

Still, he didn't let that slow him down.

He asked teachers for extra assignments. He found new books wherever he could. He wrote notes and observations in the margins, adding his own thoughts next to the printed words. And when classes were over for the day, he went right back to what he loved most—exploring plants.

Neosho had different soil, different flowers, different trees than the Carver farm. George studied them all. He spent his nights in the home of Mariah Watkins, a kind woman who let him stay in exchange for helping with chores. She saw something special in him, something that set him apart from other boys his age.

One evening, after watching him carefully examine a plant outside her house, she gave him advice he never forgot.

"Young man," she said, "you must learn all you can, then go out and give your learning back to the people."

That idea—that knowledge wasn't just for him, but for others—stuck with him.

He didn't want to learn just to be smart. He wanted to learn so he could help.

That thought stayed with him as he moved from town to town, searching for more schools, more books, more teachers. It stayed with him when he eventually found a college that would accept him, when he studied late into the night, when he worked harder than anyone else to prove he belonged.

Struggles to get an education

George Washington Carver knew that learning was his way forward. He had seen what life was like without education—hard, limited, full of obstacles that kept people from reaching their potential. He didn't want that kind of life. He wanted answers, opportunities, and a way to use knowledge to make things better. But getting an education wasn't easy.

Missouri, like many states at the time, didn't make it simple for Black children to go to school. Schools for white children were common, but schools for Black students were rare, underfunded, and often far away. If George wanted to learn, he would have to fight for it.

The school in Neosho was the closest one he could attend, but it wasn't close at all. It was about ten miles from the Carver farm—a distance far too great to walk back and forth every day. Staying home wasn't an option. There was nothing left for him to learn there.

One morning, without telling the Carvers much more than that he was leaving, he set out toward Neosho with little more than hope. He didn't have money. He didn't have a place to stay. He barely even had a plan. But he had his determination, and that was enough.

The road stretched long before him, dusty and uneven, winding past fields and woods. His legs ached, but he kept going. He had no way of knowing what would happen once he reached Neosho. What if the school turned him away? What if there was no place for him to sleep? What if no one was willing to help? These were all real possibilities, but stopping wasn't one of them.

By the time he arrived, the sun was low in the sky. Neosho wasn't a big town, but to George, it felt like a world of opportunity. The school was small, just a single-room building, and the teacher, a Black man named Stephen Frost, taught as many students as could fit inside.

George had one more problem to solve. He needed a place to stay.

That first night, he curled up in a barn, grateful for the roof over his head, even if it belonged to someone else's animals. But sleeping in a barn wasn't a long-term solution. He needed something more stable if he was going to make Neosho his new home.

A woman named Mariah Watkins, known in town for helping those in need, offered him a place to stay in exchange for chores. It wasn't much, but it was enough. She fed him, gave him a small space to sleep, and most importantly, encouraged him. She saw something in him that others had overlooked—that hunger for knowledge, that unwillingness to accept life as it was.

"You must learn all you can," she told him, "then go out and give your learning back to the people."

That advice stayed with him for the rest of his life.

Attending school was everything he had hoped for, but it wasn't easy. He didn't have proper clothes or supplies. While other children went home to families who could support them, George worked for his education. Before and after school, he swept floors, washed dishes, did farm work—anything to earn his keep.

Some students had parents who helped them with their lessons. George had no one. If he struggled to understand something, he had to figure it out on his own. He copied notes over and over, studied by candlelight, and reread the same pages until the words made sense.

He didn't let embarrassment stop him. If he didn't understand something in class, he asked questions. If there were no books available, he found someone willing to lend him one. When he ran out of books to borrow, he read newspapers, pamphlets—anything with words.

But even Neosho wasn't enough. He wanted more than a basic education.

That meant moving again, leaving behind everything familiar, and heading to a new town with new challenges. Over the next several years, he went from school to school, working his way through each one. Sometimes, he had a place to stay. Other times, he didn't.

At one point, he traveled to Fort Scott, Kansas, where he found work as a cook while attending school. But the dangers of being a Black student in a largely white town quickly became clear. One night, he witnessed a violent attack on a Black man in the street. The brutality of what he saw shook him, and he knew staying in Fort Scott wasn't safe. He left that very night, slipping out of town before dawn.

But he didn't give up.

Each time he left a school, he found another. Each time he was turned away, he kept looking. Each time he was told no, he pushed forward. He took whatever work he could find—farm labor, housework, hotel jobs—just to stay afloat.

Years passed before he finally found his way to

Highland University in Kansas, a school that, at first, accepted him. For the first time, it seemed like the door to higher education had finally opened. But when the university learned he was Black, they took back their acceptance.

That rejection could have broken him.

It didn't.

He kept going, eventually making his way to Simpson College in Iowa, where he studied art before a professor noticed his talent for science and encouraged him to switch to agriculture. That path led him to Iowa State Agricultural College, where he became the first Black student—and later, the first Black professor.

2

THE POWER OF EDUCATION

The dirt road stretched out ahead, uneven and dry, disappearing into the horizon where the morning sun had barely begun its climb. George Washington Carver had no choice but to follow it. He had left before dawn, his feet moving over familiar paths, kicking up dust with each step. The Carver farm was behind him, but the school in Neosho was still far ahead—miles away, farther than most people would ever walk in a single day. But this wasn't just a walk. It was his only chance to learn.

Each step felt like a small victory, proof that he wasn't giving up. His legs ached, but he didn't stop. The weight of his few belongings pressed against his back, a small bundle of clothes and books he had managed to gather. Some days, the road felt endless. The heat settled over him like a heavy blanket in the afternoon, making the air thick and hard to breathe. Other days, the wind was sharp and unforgiving, whipping at his skin as if trying to push him backward.

He had no shoes, at least not ones sturdy enough for the journey. His feet knew every stone and root beneath them, knew the way the ground changed from soft earth to sharp gravel. He had learned how to step carefully, how to keep moving forward even when blisters formed and the soles of his feet burned.

Stopping wasn't an option.

At first, the distance between the farm and the school seemed impossible. Walking ten miles on foot, alone, before the sun even rose, just to reach a classroom—who would do such a thing? But to George, the real question was, how could he not? Staying home meant missing out on knowledge, missing out on the answers he had spent his whole life searching for.

The world outside the farm had always fascinated him. Plants, soil, the way things grew—all of it was a mystery he wanted to solve. But he needed help. He needed books, teachers, a place where people understood the questions he was asking. That place was in Neosho, not on the Carver farm.

The road tested his determination every day. Some mornings, his stomach growled with hunger, reminding him that food was never guaranteed. He had learned how to ignore it, how to push through the emptiness until he found a meal—sometimes at school, sometimes at the kindness of strangers, sometimes not at all.

There were days when the sky opened up, drenching him in cold rain that clung to his skin, making his clothes heavy. Other days, the road was nothing but mud, sucking at his feet, trying to pull him down. And then there were the nights. If he couldn't find a place to stay, he slept wherever he could—under trees, inside barns, anywhere that offered even a little bit of shelter.

He had to be careful.

Traveling alone as a young Black boy wasn't safe. There were people who didn't think he should be walking these roads, people who believed that school wasn't meant for him. He had seen the way some towns treated Black travelers, how quickly suspicion turned into threats. He knew that at any moment, someone could try to stop him. He had no protection, no one to fight for him if things went wrong. All he had was his determination—and the knowledge that he couldn't afford to be afraid.

The miles passed slowly, but each one brought him closer to something bigger than himself. The first time he finally reached Neosho, standing outside the small schoolhouse, his feet ached and his clothes were dusty, but he didn't care. The long journey, the hunger, the exhaustion—it had all been worth it.

The classroom wasn't anything fancy. A single room, crowded with students, a teacher who did his best with what little they had. But to George, it was everything.

He sat in that classroom and listened carefully, absorbing every word. He wrote down notes, sometimes on scraps of paper, sometimes just in his mind, repeating them to himself so he wouldn't forget. Learning here meant more than just sitting at a desk. It meant proving to himself that all the walking, all the struggles, had a purpose.

When the school day ended, he didn't rush out to play like some of the other students. He found a place to sit and read, even if it was outside under the shade of a tree. His hunger could wait. His exhaustion could wait. But his curiosity never could.

The road to Neosho became part of his routine.

Each morning, he braced himself for the long walk. Each night, he found a place to rest, knowing that he would do it all over again the next day. Some people would have given up. Some would have decided that education wasn't worth this much effort.

Finding teachers and mentors who encouraged him

The teacher, Stephen Frost, stood at the front of the room, his voice carrying over the quiet murmurs of students reciting their lessons. He was a Black man, which meant he had likely fought hard for his own education before becoming a teacher. That alone made George respect him. In a world where few Black people were given the chance to read and write, teaching was a powerful thing.

George sat straight, his hands folded on his lap, waiting for the lesson to begin. He didn't want to miss a single word.

But learning wasn't just about listening. It was about asking questions, pushing beyond the words in a book, and trying to understand how things worked. While some students were content with memorizing their lessons, George wanted more. He stayed late whenever he could, hovering near Mr.

Frost's desk, asking about things that weren't even part of the day's lesson.

Most teachers might have grown tired of a student like him—one who always had another question, another idea, another way of looking at a problem. But Mr. Frost didn't. Instead, he encouraged George to keep going, to dig deeper, to think beyond what was written on the page.

"You have a mind for learning," he told him one afternoon as the other students filed out of the classroom. "Don't waste it."

That was all the encouragement George needed.

Neosho had been his first step, but he knew he couldn't stop there. If he wanted to go beyond the basics, he had to find new schools, new teachers, new places that would challenge him. That meant leaving Neosho behind. It meant walking new roads, working new jobs, and starting over in unfamiliar towns.

Not everyone was willing to help him. Many schools turned him away simply because he was Black. Some teachers refused to answer his questions, believing that a young Black boy had no reason to be so eager for knowledge.

But there were others who saw something in him.

Mariah Watkins, the woman who had given him a place to stay in Neosho, was one of them. She wasn't a teacher in the traditional sense—she didn't stand in front of a classroom or assign homework. But she taught George something just as important as reading and writing. She taught him about purpose.

She watched the way he devoured books, how he spent hours studying plants and soil, how he never seemed satisfied with simple answers. And one evening, as they sat on her porch, she gave him advice that would stay with him forever.

"You must learn all you can," she said, her voice steady and firm, "then go out and give your learning back to the people."

It wasn't just about knowledge. It was about what he did with it.

That idea followed him as he traveled from town to town, finding teachers who would guide him and mentors who would push him further.

One of them was Etta Budd, an instructor at Simpson College in Iowa. By the time George reached Simpson, he had already worked his way through multiple schools, taking whatever odd jobs he could find to pay for books and tuition. At first, he studied art—his ability to draw and paint plants in stunning detail had caught the attention of those around him.

But Miss Budd saw something else in him. She noticed that his drawings weren't just about beauty. They were about science. He wasn't sketching flowers just to make them look pretty—he was studying them, trying to capture every detail, every part of their structure. She encouraged him to take a different path, one that focused on plants not as artwork but as something to be understood and used to help people.

That conversation changed everything.

He transferred to Iowa State Agricultural College, where he met more mentors—professors who recognized his talent and drive. He wasn't just a student who memorized facts and repeated them back. He was a thinker, a problem-solver, someone who saw connections where others didn't.

His professors challenged him, giving him difficult problems to solve, pushing him beyond what was expected. But instead of feeling overwhelmed, he thrived.

When he struggled, he didn't quit. When others doubted him, he worked harder. And when someone believed in him—really believed in him—he didn't let them down.

Attending College

The journey to college wasn't smooth, but George Washington Carver had never expected it to be. Getting an education had always been a fight—one he was willing to take on. He had walked miles just to attend school in Neosho. He had traveled from town to town, looking for places that would accept him. He had faced rejection and hardship at every step. But giving up had never been an option.

By the time he reached Simpson College in Indianola, Iowa, he had already spent years proving that education was worth any struggle. The moment he stepped onto the campus, he felt the same hunger he had always felt—the need to learn, to understand, to ask the questions that others overlooked. But this time, things were different.

Simpson College wasn't a school for farming. It wasn't a place where students learned about soil and crops. It was a small school, mostly focused on the arts and humanities. That was fine with George. He had always been talented at drawing, especially when it came to plants and flowers. Art, in many ways, was just another way to study nature, another way to capture the beauty of the world around him.

His sketches were detailed, almost scientific in

their precision. He didn't just draw a flower—he mapped out its petals, its leaves, the veins running through each delicate structure. His paintings weren't just pretty; they were careful studies of living things.

One of his instructors, a woman named Etta Budd, noticed something special about his work. She could see that his drawings were different. They weren't just about creating something beautiful; they were about understanding how things worked. And that made her wonder.

"Have you ever thought about studying agriculture?" she asked him one day.

The question caught George off guard. Agriculture? He had grown up surrounded by farming. He had spent his childhood watching crops grow, tending gardens, testing soil. He had spent hours studying plants—not because he had to, but because he wanted to. But until that moment, he had never thought of it as something he could study at a university.

Etta Budd saw his potential before he did. She knew that his talent for observing nature could be used for something bigger.

She encouraged him to transfer to Iowa State Agricultural College, a school known for science, farming, and research. It was a bold suggestion. At the time, no Black student had ever attended Iowa State. The idea of someone like George studying alongside white students was almost unheard of. But he had spent his whole life pushing past barriers, and he wasn't about to stop now.

It wasn't easy to get accepted. He had to prove himself, again and again. He had to work harder than anyone else, knowing that every step forward was another challenge. But when he was finally admitted, he became the first Black student at the school.

Iowa State was a different world. The classes were harder, the expectations higher. Science wasn't just about curiosity anymore—it was about formulas, experiments, research. But George thrived. He spent hours in the laboratory, testing soils, examining plants, and taking notes on every experiment he ran. His professors quickly noticed his dedication.

One of them, a professor named Louis Pammel, became a mentor to him. He saw George's talent and helped guide him, giving him opportunities that many students never received. With his encouragement, George not only studied agriculture, but also began working as a researcher at the university.

That research would change everything.

He discovered that overused soil—soil that had been planted with cotton year after year—lost its nutrients. It became dry, lifeless, unable to grow strong crops. But when farmers planted different crops, like peanuts and sweet potatoes, the soil regained its strength. This discovery was more than just science—it was a way to help poor farmers, people who were struggling to grow enough food to survive.

Becoming the first Black student and later the first Black professor at Iowa State

Walking onto that campus wasn't just a personal achievement. It was history being made.

The other students looked at him. Some with curiosity, some with doubt. Many had never studied alongside a Black student before. Some believed he didn't belong there. They whispered about him, sometimes loud enough for him to hear.

But George had learned long ago that what other people thought didn't matter as much as what he did next. He hadn't come this far just to give up because of a few stares.

The classes were harder than anything he had

ever faced. Science wasn't just about growing plants anymore—it was chemistry, biology, and mathematics all mixed together. The professors spoke quickly, expecting students to keep up. The textbooks were dense, packed with information, filled with terms he had never heard before.

Many students had grown up in wealthy families, with private tutors and libraries full of books at home. George had none of that. But he had something even more valuable: determination.

He studied harder than anyone else. While other students relaxed in the evenings, he spent hours in the lab, testing soil samples and running experiments. He asked more questions than his classmates, always eager to understand more. If something didn't make sense, he didn't let it go until he found an answer.

His professors noticed.

One of them, Dr. Louis Pammel, saw his potential right away. He saw how George stayed late after class, how he took meticulous notes, how he never seemed satisfied with just memorizing facts—he wanted to understand them.

Dr. Pammel took him under his wing, inviting him to work in the laboratory, giving him extra assignments, pushing him to think even deeper about agriculture and science. With his guidance, George started researching something that had been troubling farmers for years: why certain crops drained the soil and left the land unusable.

His research led to groundbreaking discoveries.

He found that cotton, a crop planted over and over again in the South, was exhausting the soil, stripping it of nutrients. Farmers were struggling. Land that had once produced abundant crops was now dry and barren. But George's experiments showed that planting different crops—like peanuts and sweet potatoes—could bring the soil back to life.

These discoveries weren't just about science. They were about survival.

His work was so impressive that Iowa State asked him to stay—not just as a student, but as a professor and researcher. He became the first Black faculty member in the school's history, teaching classes, guiding students, and continuing his research.

Becoming a professor wasn't just about standing in front of a classroom. It meant proving, again and again, that he had earned his place. Some students didn't want to take lessons from a Black teacher. Some questioned whether he was qualified, despite his obvious brilliance.

George responded the only way he knew how—by working harder, by teaching with passion, by making discoveries that no one could ignore.

His classrooms weren't just lectures and notes. He made science come alive, showing students how the land worked, why crops thrived or failed, and how farmers could use knowledge to grow more food, take better care of the soil, and improve their livelihoods.

3

A SCIENTIST WITH A MISSION

Booker T. Washington, the founder of Tuskegee Institute in Alabama, had heard about Carver's research and teaching. He had read about the discoveries that could help struggling farmers, especially in the South, where former enslaved people were trying to make a living off land that had been overworked for generations. Washington saw something special in Carver—someone who wasn't just a scientist, but a teacher, a problem solver, a man who could make a difference.

Would he come to Tuskegee to teach?

Carver had a choice to make. He had a secure position at Iowa State, where he was respected and had access to advanced laboratories and resources.

He could have stayed, continuing his research in a well-equipped setting. But that wasn't enough.

His discoveries weren't meant to sit in books or laboratories. They were meant to be used. They were meant to help people—especially the farmers who needed them the most.

Alabama was a world away from Iowa, and not just in distance. Tuskegee Institute was still growing, still struggling in some ways. There were no modern laboratories. No fancy equipment. No endless rows of books waiting in a university library. It was a school built for Black students, many of whom had never been given a real chance to learn.

Carver knew what that felt like.

Packing up his life wasn't easy, but he didn't hesitate. He left behind Iowa, the only home he had really known since leaving Missouri, and made the long journey south to Alabama, where new challenges—and new opportunities—were waiting.

The moment he stepped onto the campus of Tuskegee, he saw what Booker T. Washington had seen: students eager to learn, but with little to work with. The school was young, the buildings were simple, and the resources were limited. There were no well-stocked labs filled with microscopes and chemicals. There were no gleaming greenhouses for experiments.

None of that mattered.

He had spent his whole life making the most of what he had. He had studied plants by walking through fields, tested soil with nothing more than his hands, and learned without proper books or supplies. If he had done it, these students could too.

His first job was to set up an agriculture program from almost nothing. He wasn't just a teacher—he was a builder, a fixer, a creator. He gathered whatever materials he could find. He turned an old chicken coop into his first lab, using wooden tables and whatever tools were available. His students helped him gather plants, soil, and scraps of equipment. Together, they built something out of nothing.

Carver's classes weren't like other science lessons. He didn't just lecture from a book. He took his students outside, showing them how the land worked, how soil could be healed, how crops could be grown better. He didn't want them to just memorize facts—he wanted them to understand, to see the connections between science and everyday life.

Word spread quickly. Farmers, some who had been enslaved just a few decades earlier, came to hear him speak. They were struggling. Their cotton fields were failing. Their soil was dry and lifeless. Their crops weren't growing the way they once had.

Carver didn't just tell them what to do—he showed them. He demonstrated how rotating crops—planting peanuts or sweet potatoes instead of cotton—could restore the soil. He taught them how to make their own fertilizers when they couldn't afford expensive ones. He found ways to help them grow food to feed their families, instead of relying on a single cash crop that could fail.

His work wasn't about getting rich or becoming famous. He refused to patent many of his discoveries because he believed knowledge should be shared, not sold. His mission was simple: to help people survive, to give them the tools to improve their own lives.

Helping poor farmers improve their crops

The land in the South was tired. Fields that once stretched green with healthy cotton plants were now dry, cracked, and lifeless. Farmers—many of them newly freed Black men and women—were struggling to grow enough to survive. They had been told to plant cotton, year after year, because it was the only crop that could bring in money. But now, their fields were failing.

George Washington Carver had seen these problems long before he ever stepped foot in Alabama. He had spent years studying soil, testing crops, and trying to understand what made land rich or barren. When he arrived at Tuskegee Institute, he didn't just see a school. He saw an opportunity to help people.

His students were not just young men looking for an education. They were future farmers, future leaders in their communities. Many of them came from families that had worked the land for generations but had never been given the tools to succeed. Carver wasn't just teaching them how to farm. He was teaching them how to survive.

The first thing he told them was something most of them had never heard before: The problem wasn't the weather or bad luck. The problem was the soil itself.

Cotton had drained the nutrients from the earth, leaving behind fields that couldn't support crops anymore. If farmers kept planting cotton, year after year, things would only get worse. But there was a way to fix it.

Carver had spent years researching crop rotation—the idea that planting different crops could restore the soil. Instead of planting cotton over and over again, farmers could grow peanuts, sweet potatoes, cowpeas, and pecans. These plants put nutrients back into the soil, making it fertile again.

Most farmers didn't believe him at first. Cotton was all they knew. It was what their fathers and grandfathers had grown. It was what the landowners expected them to plant. Switching to peanuts or sweet potatoes seemed risky. How would they sell them? How would they survive if no one wanted to buy anything but cotton?

Carver understood their fears, and he didn't blame them. Changing old ways was never easy. That was why he didn't just tell them what to do—he showed them.

He set up experimental farms at Tuskegee, where students tested different crops. He gave lectures, traveling from town to town, speaking to farmers in churches, in schoolhouses, even out in the fields where they worked. He demonstrated how crop rotation worked, digging his hands into the soil, showing them the difference between dead land and healthy land.

But Carver didn't stop at just fixing the soil. He

wanted to make sure farmers could make a living. What was the point of growing peanuts if no one wanted to buy them? What would they do with all those sweet potatoes?

That was when he started developing new uses for these crops. He found ways to turn peanuts into oils, paints, and soaps. He experimented with sweet potatoes, creating flour, glue, rubber, and even a type of paper. If farmers couldn't sell their crops in traditional ways, they could use them to make products that people needed.

He refused to take credit for these inventions. He refused to make money from them. He believed that knowledge should be shared freely. He wanted poor farmers to benefit, not just businessmen or factory owners.

Farmers who followed his advice saw their land start to heal. Their fields turned green again. They had more food to eat. They had new ways to make a living.

Understanding the problem with soil depletion

Everywhere he traveled in the South, he saw the same problem. Fields that had once been full of life were now dry, cracked, and weak. Farmers were struggling to grow enough crops to survive. Their cotton plants were smaller, their harvests were shrinking, and no matter how hard they worked, the soil refused to give them what it once had.

He knew what was happening before they did.

The land was exhausted.

For years, farmers had been planting the same crop—cotton—over and over again. Cotton was valuable. It was what landowners expected, what the markets demanded, what generations of farmers had always grown. But no one had ever stopped to ask what cotton was doing to the soil itself.

Carver had spent years studying how plants and soil worked together. He had examined soil under microscopes, tested different types of crops, and watched what happened when land was used the same way for too long. He had seen the difference between healthy soil and soil that had been stripped of everything it needed to sustain life.

And now, he was seeing the results on a massive scale.

Soil depletion wasn't something farmers could see right away. It was a slow process, happening over years. Each time a cotton plant was harvested, it took nutrients from the soil. But because farmers kept replanting cotton and nothing else, those nutrients were never replaced. Year after year, the soil became weaker, unable to provide what the crops needed.

At first, the changes were small—cotton plants weren't as tall, leaves weren't as green, flowers weren't as full. But over time, the plants struggled more and more. Yields dropped. The cotton wasn't as strong. The land, once rich and fertile, was now dry and lifeless.

Farmers didn't understand what was happening. Many of them thought they just needed to work harder, to plow deeper, to plant more seeds. But no matter how much effort they put in, the problem only got worse.

Carver knew the solution wasn't harder work. It was smarter work.

If soil could be exhausted, that meant it could also be restored. The key was to stop taking from the land without giving something back.

He started talking to farmers, trying to explain what was happening beneath their feet. He told them that soil wasn't just dirt—it was a living system, full of nutrients that plants needed to grow. He showed them how different crops affected the soil in different ways.

Some plants, like cotton, drained the soil. Others, like peanuts, sweet potatoes, and legumes, did the opposite—they restored nutrients, bringing life back to the land. If farmers planted these crops in between cotton seasons, the soil would recover.

Many didn't believe him at first. They had spent their whole lives growing cotton, just like their parents and grandparents had before them. They didn't see how something as simple as planting a different crop could make a difference.

But Carver was patient. He demonstrated the process, planting peanuts in worn-out fields, then showing how the soil became rich and fertile again. He let the results speak for themselves.

Once they saw the change with their own eyes, farmers started to listen.

Teaching crop rotation

George Washington Carver knew that if farmers kept planting cotton year after year, the soil would never recover. The land had been drained of its nutrients, and unless something changed, the problem would only get worse. But knowing the solution wasn't enough—he had to convince farmers to actually try something new.

That wasn't easy.

Many of the farmers he spoke to had been

growing cotton for generations. It was all they knew. They didn't own their land; they rented it from white landowners who expected cotton to be planted because it was the crop that made money. The idea of planting peanuts, sweet potatoes, or cowpeas instead? That sounded like a waste of time.

Carver wasn't one to give up. He had spent his whole life learning, experimenting, and proving that science could help people. Now, his challenge was to take everything he had discovered about soil and crops and make it simple enough for struggling farmers to use in their daily lives.

He started with his students at Tuskegee Institute, turning them into both learners and teachers. He took them out into the fields, showing them the difference between exhausted soil and healthy soil. He dug his fingers into the dirt and explained why certain crops took nutrients while others put nutrients back. He had them plant different seeds and observe what happened over time.

But it wasn't enough to teach only the students in his classrooms. The farmers—the ones who were out there every day working the land—needed to see it for themselves.

Carver traveled across the South, meeting with farmers in small towns and rural fields. He didn't wait for them to come to him—he went straight to them. He stood in front of groups of men who had spent their whole lives in the dirt and explained, in simple terms, what was happening to their land.

"You don't have to give up on cotton," he told them, "but you have to give your soil a chance to breathe."

He showed them how planting peanuts or sweet potatoes one season and then cotton the next would bring life back to the soil. He explained how cowpeas could act as natural fertilizer, putting nitrogen back into the dirt. He taught them how to make compost from leftover plant material instead of letting it go to waste.

Still, many were hesitant. They had mouths to feed and little time to take risks. If peanuts didn't sell, if sweet potatoes didn't bring in money, what would they do?

Carver had an answer for that, too.

He didn't just teach farmers how to restore their land—he showed them new ways to use the crops they planted. He experimented with peanuts, creating dozens of products from peanut oil to soap. He found ways to turn sweet potatoes into flour, rubber, and even glue. If farmers couldn't sell their crops raw, they could turn them into something useful.

Word spread. More and more farmers began testing his ideas, and when they saw their soil improving, they taught their neighbors. Slowly, the land started to recover. Fields that had once been dry and useless began producing food again.

4

THE MANY USES OF PEANUTS

If there's one thing most people think they know about George Washington Carver, it's that he invented peanut butter. It's been repeated in books, in classrooms, and even on TV. But here's the truth: he didn't.

Peanut butter existed long before Carver started experimenting with peanuts. In fact, people had been making pastes out of ground nuts for centuries. The ancient Aztecs and Incas were mashing roasted peanuts into a paste long before the United States even existed. Later, in the 1800s, inventors in Canada and the U.S. created machines to grind peanuts into a smooth, spreadable form. By the time Carver was doing his research, peanut butter was already being sold in stores.

So, if he didn't invent peanut butter, why do so many people believe he did?

The answer lies in the work he actually *did* do with peanuts—because even though he didn't invent peanut butter, he discovered over 300 other uses for peanuts that changed the way people thought about the crop.

Carver wasn't interested in peanuts because he wanted a new sandwich topping. He was trying to solve a problem. Farmers in the South were struggling. Cotton had destroyed their soil, and they needed new crops to plant—crops that could bring life back to the land and still make them money. Peanuts were one of the answers. They grew well in poor soil, added nutrients back into the ground, and could be used for more than just eating.

Carver wanted to prove to farmers that peanuts weren't just a snack. He wanted to show them that they could be turned into useful products that people needed. So, he got to work.

In his laboratory at Tuskegee Institute, Carver tested and experimented, finding ways to transform peanuts into entirely new things. He developed peanut-based soap, peanut ink, peanut glue, peanut oil, and even peanut rubber. He figured out how to use peanuts to make plastics, cosmetics, and medicines. Some of these ideas took off, while others never made it past the lab. But his point was clear—peanuts weren't just food; they were a resource with endless possibilities.

As Carver's fame grew, people started connecting his name with peanuts more and more. He gave presentations about his work, showing off the many uses he had discovered. Newspapers and magazines wrote about him, calling him the "Peanut Man." But somewhere along the way, his discoveries were exaggerated.

Instead of saying he found new ways to use peanuts, people started saying he *invented* peanut butter. It was a mistake that stuck.

Carver himself never claimed to have created peanut butter. He corrected people when they got it wrong. He was proud of his peanut research, but he always wanted people to understand the bigger picture. To him, peanuts were never the most important thing—helping farmers survive was.

Despite all his work, Carver didn't make any money from his peanut discoveries. He never patented them because he believed that knowledge should be shared freely. He didn't want people to buy his inventions; he wanted them to use his ideas to improve their own lives.

The peanut butter myth might not be true, but that doesn't take away from what Carver actually accomplished. He helped struggling farmers, changed agriculture in the South, and proved that science could solve real problems. His work wasn't about taking credit—it was about making a difference.

And that's exactly what he did.

Discovering over 300 uses for peanuts, including paints, oils, and soaps

Discovering Over 300 Uses for Peanuts, Including Paints, Oils, and Soaps

George Washington Carver never looked at a peanut and saw just a snack. Where others saw something small and simple, he saw endless possibilities. Peanuts, like people, had potential far beyond what most believed. And Carver was determined to prove it.

At Tuskegee Institute, his laboratory wasn't filled with expensive equipment or fancy tools. He worked with what he had—basic glass beakers, makeshift test tubes, and a deep understanding of chemistry and agriculture. His goal wasn't to impress other scientists. His goal was to help farmers, to give them ways to use peanuts that went beyond selling them raw. If peanuts could be turned into useful products, struggling farmers might have a new way to earn a living.

Carver started with simple questions. Could peanuts be used for something other than food? Could their oils be extracted and turned into something valuable? Could the proteins inside them be changed into new materials? Every experiment led to another, and each answer brought new ideas.

One of his earliest successes was peanut oil. He discovered that pressing peanuts could extract a light, clean oil that could be used for cooking, but that wasn't all. The oil was also useful for polishing furniture, treating leather, and even soothing sore muscles. Carver believed peanut oil could have medical benefits, and he used it to massage patients who suffered from polio, hoping it would ease their symptoms.

But he didn't stop there.

Next came peanut-based soaps. He found that the natural fats inside peanuts could be used to create a smooth, cleansing soap that worked just as well as the expensive ones sold in stores. For farmers who couldn't afford luxury items, this was a game-changer. They could grow peanuts, press out the oils, and make their own soap at home.

Then there was peanut-based paint. Carver experimented with different ways to mix peanut extracts with natural dyes, creating a paint that was both durable and affordable. At a time when materials were expensive, this discovery gave farmers another way to use their peanut crops.

The list kept growing. Peanut ink. Peanut glue. Peanut rubber. Peanut-based plastics. Carver tested and retested, always asking himself, "What else can this be?"

His work attracted attention far beyond Alabama. Businesses wanted to know if his peanut discoveries could be mass-produced. Government officials were curious about whether peanut oil could replace other oils in manufacturing. Even Henry Ford, the famous carmaker, invited Carver to his factory to discuss the potential for peanut-based materials in the automobile industry.

His work with sweet potatoes and other crops

Peanuts may have made George Washington Carver famous, but they weren't the only crop he studied. Sweet potatoes, pecans, cowpeas, and other plants all became part of his research. He believed that farming wasn't just about growing food—it was about understanding the land, using resources wisely, and finding new ways to make crops valuable beyond the dinner table.

Sweet potatoes, in particular, fascinated him. Like peanuts, they grew well in poor soil, meaning they could help farmers rebuild their land after years of cotton planting. But sweet potatoes had a problem: most people only thought of them as food. If farmers planted fields full of sweet potatoes, what could they do with them besides eat them? How could they turn them into something useful?

Carver started experimenting, breaking down sweet potatoes in his Tuskegee laboratory the same way he had done with peanuts. He wanted to know what else they could become.

One of his first discoveries was sweet potato flour. Regular wheat flour could be expensive, and some farmers didn't have access to it at all. But Carver found that sweet potatoes could be dried and ground into a fine powder, making an alternative that could be used for baking bread, biscuits, and cakes. For families who couldn't afford store-bought flour, this was a way to make their own.

Then there was sweet potato starch. Carver

figured out how to extract starch from sweet potatoes and turn it into glue. He tested it himself, finding that it worked just as well as the glue sold in stores. Schools with limited supplies could use it for paper projects, and farmers could make their own rather than buying expensive glue.

The experiments continued. Sweet potato ink. Sweet potato rubber. Sweet potato paper. He found ways to make synthetic rubber using sweet potatoes, a discovery that caught the attention of scientists and businesses. During World War II, when rubber supplies were running low, the U.S. government looked into Carver's research as a possible solution.

His discoveries weren't just about replacing store-bought items. He wanted to make farming more sustainable, to show people that the land could provide more than they thought.

But sweet potatoes weren't his only focus.

He encouraged farmers to grow cowpeas, which, like peanuts, helped restore nutrients to the soil. He studied pecans, looking at their nutritional value and finding ways to use them beyond just eating. He even experimented with wild plants, always searching for new ways to use what nature provided.

Promoting self-sufficiency for farmers

George Washington Carver didn't just want to help farmers grow better crops—he wanted to help them build better lives. Farming was more than planting seeds and waiting for them to grow. It was about survival, about making sure families had food to eat, goods to sell, and a future that didn't depend on things beyond their control.

Many of the farmers he worked with were poor. Some had once been enslaved. Others were sharecroppers, farming land that wasn't even theirs, forced to give a portion of their harvest to landowners. They had little money, little power, and few choices. Carver wanted to change that.

He believed that farmers didn't have to rely on big companies or expensive products to succeed. They didn't need to buy costly fertilizers, pesticides, or store-bought goods when they could make many of these things themselves. He wanted them to be self-sufficient—to have the knowledge and skills to provide for their families without depending on outside forces that might fail them.

His first step was education.

Carver knew that many farmers had never been given the chance to go to school. They didn't have access to books, scientific studies, or the latest agricultural advancements. He made it his mission to bring that knowledge directly to them.

At Tuskegee Institute, he started what became known as the "Jesup Wagon"—a traveling school on wheels. He and his students loaded up supplies, samples of soil, different types of crops, and simple tools. Then, they took to the road, traveling from farm to farm, town to town, teaching farmers how to improve their land.

They showed them how to enrich their soil with compost instead of buying expensive fertilizers. They taught them to rotate crops, planting peanuts or sweet potatoes one season to restore the land before growing cotton again. They explained how to make their own soap, dyes, paints, and even paper from farm resources instead of spending money at the store.

Carver didn't just lecture—he demonstrated. He dug his hands into the soil, showing farmers what healthy dirt should feel like. He crushed sweet potatoes in his hands, explaining how they could be turned into flour or used to make glue. He boiled peanut oil over a fire, turning it into a smooth polish for furniture. He let the farmers touch, see, and smell the results for themselves.

He also encouraged them to stop relying so much on cotton. Cotton was an unpredictable crop. Some years it sold for high prices, and other years, it left farmers in debt. He urged them to grow crops that they could eat, like peanuts, sweet potatoes, and pecans—things that would provide food for their families even if they couldn't sell them.

Many farmers had never thought of growing crops for anything other than profit. But Carver reminded them that a farm that could feed itself was a farm that could survive hard times.

His message spread. Farmers who had struggled for years began to see improvements in their land and their lives. They started planting a variety of crops. They learned how to preserve food for the winter. They discovered that they could make everyday products from what they grew instead of spending what little money they had.

5

CARVER'S IMPACT BEYOND THE FARM

George Washington Carver believed that farming wasn't just about growing crops—it was about taking care of the land, ensuring that it could provide for future generations. He had spent years teaching farmers how to make their soil healthier, how to grow more than just cotton, and how to become self-sufficient. But his vision stretched far beyond individual farms. He wanted to change the way people thought about agriculture itself.

Many farmers in the South had been using the same farming methods for generations. They planted the same crops year after year, plowed their fields deeply, and relied on chemical fertilizers when their soil began to fail. Carver saw the damage this was doing. Fields were being worn out. Rain was washing away valuable topsoil. Farms that had once thrived were becoming barren.

He spoke out against these harmful practices, urging farmers to think differently. He encouraged them to farm with the future in mind—to use methods that would keep their land productive not just for one season, but for many years to come.

One of the biggest changes he promoted was crop rotation. Instead of exhausting the soil with cotton year after year, he taught farmers to alternate their crops. Planting peanuts, sweet potatoes, or cowpeas in between cotton seasons restored nutrients to the land. This simple change made a huge difference.

But sustainable agriculture wasn't just about soil —it was about making the most of what the land had to offer. Carver encouraged farmers to plant a variety of crops instead of relying on just one. He showed them how different plants could work together, how trees could prevent soil erosion, and how composting could naturally fertilize the land without expensive chemicals.

He also taught them to pay attention to the environment. If the land was dry, they needed to plant crops that required less water. If an area was prone to erosion, they needed to use plants with deep roots to hold the soil in place. Farming wasn't just about taking from the land—it was about giving back to it.

Working with Booker T. Washington at Tuskegee

George Washington Carver had spent years searching for places where he could learn. Now, for the first time, he had found a place where he could teach. Tuskegee Institute in Alabama wasn't just a school—it was a mission. And at the center of that mission was its founder, Booker T. Washington.

Washington had built Tuskegee from the ground up. He believed that education was the key to helping Black Americans move forward, but not just any education. He wanted students to learn practical skills—things they could use to build businesses, improve their farms, and create better lives for themselves and their families. He saw college not just as a place for books and lectures, but as a training ground for real-world success.

That's why he wanted Carver.

Carver had turned down offers from other schools, even from businesses that wanted to hire him as a scientist. He wasn't interested in making money or gaining fame. He wanted to help people.

When Washington wrote to him, inviting him to come teach agriculture at Tuskegee, Carver saw it as an opportunity to do exactly that.

His journey to Alabama was long, and when he arrived, he saw right away that Tuskegee was nothing like the big universities he had known. It didn't have fancy laboratories or endless supplies. Some of the classrooms were little more than wooden shacks. Students built many of the buildings themselves, learning carpentry and construction as part of their education. Money was tight. Resources were limited.

Carver didn't complain. He had spent his whole life making do with what he had. If he didn't have the equipment he needed, he would figure out another way.

At first, his job was simple: teach agriculture. But Carver didn't just want to teach his students how to farm—he wanted to show them how to farm better. He took them out into the fields, digging into the soil, explaining why land became exhausted and how it could be restored. He taught them about crop rotation, composting, and using plants in ways they had never considered before.

His students weren't the only ones who needed these lessons. The farmers surrounding Tuskegee were struggling. Their cotton fields were failing. They didn't know how to fix their soil, how to grow anything else, or how to make a living beyond cotton. Carver saw that his job wasn't just inside the classroom—it was out in the fields, in the farming communities, wherever people needed guidance.

Washington supported Carver's efforts, but their relationship wasn't always easy. Washington was a leader, a man who had spent his life fighting for education and opportunities for Black Americans. He expected discipline, order, and strict schedules. Carver, on the other hand, was a scientist who needed time for experiments, research, and long hours in the lab.

At times, Washington pushed Carver to do more administrative work—raising money for the school, handling paperwork, attending meetings. Carver hated this part of the job. He didn't want to sit in an office; he wanted to be outside, working with his students, making discoveries that could help farmers.

Despite their differences, they respected each other. Washington knew that Carver's work was essential, and Carver knew that Tuskegee wouldn't exist without Washington's leadership. They had different approaches, but the same goal: lifting up their people through education and hard work.

Carver stayed at Tuskegee for the rest of his life. Even after Washington passed away, even when other schools and organizations tried to lure him away with better salaries and bigger labs, he remained. Tuskegee was his home, and its students were his family.

Meeting famous people

George Washington Carver never sought fame. He never cared about making money from his discoveries, and he didn't chase after awards or recognition. He wanted his work to help everyday people—farmers, students, and families struggling to survive. But when someone makes a difference as big as Carver did, people start to notice.

And some of the people who noticed were among the most powerful in the world.

One day, a letter arrived at Tuskegee Institute. It was from the White House. The president of the United States, Theodore Roosevelt, had heard about Carver's agricultural research. He had read about the work being done to improve farming in the

South and was particularly interested in Carver's discoveries about peanuts.

Roosevelt wanted advice.

This was 1904, and the United States was dealing with a problem—finding ways to grow and produce more food for a rapidly growing country. Roosevelt, known for his curiosity and admiration for scientists, had been told that Carver might have the answers he was looking for.

Most people would have been overwhelmed at the idea of being summoned by the president, but Carver treated it the same way he treated everything else: as an opportunity to teach. He traveled to Washington, D.C., and sat down with Roosevelt to discuss agriculture, peanuts, and how America could improve its food supply.

The president listened. He asked questions. Carver answered with the patience of a teacher explaining something to a student. And by the end of the meeting, Roosevelt was convinced—Carver's work was important, and more people needed to hear about it.

That meeting led to something unexpected: the government started paying closer attention to Carver's ideas. Roosevelt later arranged for Carver to serve as an agricultural adviser, helping to shape policies that supported better farming practices across the country.

But Roosevelt wasn't the only famous person who wanted to learn from Carver.

A few years later, another letter arrived, this time from a man who was changing the world in a different way: Henry Ford.

Ford wasn't a politician. He was an inventor and businessman, the man behind the Ford Motor Company. He had revolutionized the automobile industry, making cars affordable for the average person by using assembly line production. But Ford wasn't just interested in cars—he was interested in science, agriculture, and new ways of using plants to create materials.

And he had heard that Carver was the man to talk to.

Ford invited Carver to visit his factory in Michigan. It was a long way from the farms of Alabama, but Carver saw it as another chance to share what he had learned. When he arrived, Ford showed him around, explaining how he was looking for ways to make car parts using plant-based materials instead of metal.

Carver was fascinated. He had already been experimenting with peanut-based plastics and other alternative materials. He and Ford discussed the idea of using peanuts and soybeans to create rubber for tires and other car parts. Ford even built a special laboratory dedicated to agricultural research, inspired by Carver's work.

The two men developed a deep respect for each other. Ford admired Carver's dedication to science and education. Carver admired Ford's ability to turn ideas into real-world solutions. Over the years, they remained in contact, exchanging ideas and discussing ways that science and industry could work together.

His efforts to improve racial relations through science

Racial divisions were deep in America, especially in the South. Carver had lived through slavery as a child, and even after it was abolished, he had seen how Black people were denied opportunities, treated unfairly, and often left to struggle on their own. He had spent his life pushing past those barriers, proving that knowledge and hard work could open doors. But he didn't just want success for himself—he wanted a world where people of all races could work together.

For Carver, science was a bridge.

He knew that facts and discoveries didn't care about the color of someone's skin. A good farming method worked for everyone, no matter who they were. A new invention could benefit the whole world, not just one group of people. If Black and white farmers could see that they had the same problems—and that the solutions helped them both—it might change the way they saw each other.

He traveled to farming communities across the South, speaking to both Black and white farmers about improving soil and growing better crops. At a time when racial tensions were high, this was no small thing. Many white farmers weren't used to listening to a Black scientist, and some refused to at first. But Carver wasn't there to argue or demand respect—he was there to teach.

He won people over with his knowledge, his patience, and his willingness to help anyone who was willing to learn. Slowly, he gained respect in places where Black men were often ignored.

One of the ways he built connections was through his work with peanuts and other crops. His discoveries were useful to both Black and white communities, and businesses began to take notice. Some of his biggest supporters were white businessmen and scientists who saw the value in what he was doing. Henry Ford, for example, didn't just admire Carver's scientific mind—he saw him as a friend.

Carver was invited to speak at conferences, where he addressed audiences that were often mostly white. He spoke about science, about agriculture, about the importance of education, but he also spoke about something deeper: unity.

He never spoke with anger about racism, even though he had every reason to. Instead, he encouraged people to work together, to lift each other up, to find common ground through science and education. He believed that showing kindness and intelligence was the best way to break down barriers.

6

HIS LEGACY LIVES ON

At first, Carver's work was recognized mostly by farmers, students, and scientists. They saw the difference he was making. He had taught poor farmers how to revive their soil, helped communities become more self-sufficient, and created hundreds of new uses for crops that had once been overlooked. People admired him not just for his intelligence, but for his kindness and humility.

Then, more powerful people started paying attention.

In 1916, Carver was invited to join the Royal Society of Arts in London, one of the most respected scientific organizations in the world. It was rare for an American to be given such an honor, and even rarer for a Black scientist. This recognition showed that his research wasn't just helping farmers in the South—it was making an impact on a global scale.

A few years later, in 1921, Carver was asked to speak before the United States Congress. Not many people got this kind of opportunity, but his discoveries with peanuts had drawn national attention. Congress was considering new tariffs on imported peanuts, and peanut farmers in the U.S. wanted to prove that peanuts were an important crop. Who better to explain their value than the man who had discovered over 300 uses for them?

Carver stood before the lawmakers in Washington, D.C., and spoke about all the ways peanuts could be used—peanut oil, peanut soap, peanut rubber, peanut ink. He didn't just list facts; he held their attention, demonstrating his passion for science and agriculture. By the time he finished, the room had gone silent. Then, applause filled the chamber. The lawmakers were amazed. One congressman reportedly stood up and said, "We didn't know peanuts were so important!"

After that, Carver became more well-known than ever.

In 1923, he was awarded the Spingarn Medal from the NAACP, one of the highest honors given to

Black Americans. The award recognized not only his scientific achievements but also his role as a teacher and leader. He had become a symbol of perseverance, someone who had risen from slavery to become one of the most respected scientists in the country.

Carver could have used this attention to demand a higher salary or to ask for money for his research. But he didn't. He continued to live simply, wearing the same old suits, waking up before dawn to work in his lab, and spending his days teaching at Tuskegee. He still believed that knowledge should be shared freely.

As his fame grew, invitations poured in. He was asked to meet President Calvin Coolidge. He visited Henry Ford's factories and talked with business leaders about how agriculture and industry could work together. In 1939, he received the Roosevelt Medal for his contributions to science and humanitarian work.

His simple life and belief in helping others

George Washington Carver could have been a rich man. He could have made a fortune from his discoveries—selling his peanut-based products, patenting his sweet potato inventions, or working for big companies that wanted his ideas. But he didn't.

Money never interested him.

He lived in a small, modest room on the Tuskegee Institute campus. His furniture was simple, his clothes were plain, and his daily routine never changed much. He woke up before dawn, often at four in the morning, and spent the first hours of the day in prayer and meditation. Then, he went to his laboratory or his classroom, where he spent the rest of his time working, teaching, and experimenting.

He never owned a car. When he had to travel, he often walked or accepted rides from friends and students. He ate little—mostly fruits, nuts, and vegetables. Some days, he skipped meals entirely, saying he didn't need much to keep going. He refused to waste anything, whether it was food, paper, or supplies.

Carver believed that life wasn't about wealth or possessions. To him, true success wasn't measured in money but in how much a person could help others. That belief shaped everything he did.

At Tuskegee, his students quickly realized that their professor wasn't like other scientists. He didn't just want them to memorize facts—he wanted them to understand how to use their knowledge to serve others. He encouraged them to study agriculture not for profit but to help struggling farmers. He taught them that education wasn't just about bettering themselves but about improving the lives of their families and communities.

Outside of the classroom, he gave his time freely. Farmers came to him for advice, and he always made time to listen. Some couldn't afford to pay for supplies, so he helped them find ways to make do with what they had. When local families needed medicine, he experimented with plants to find natural remedies that could relieve pain and heal wounds. If someone was sick, he sat with them. If someone was struggling, he offered guidance.

He believed that everything he learned was meant to be shared. That's why he never patented most of his inventions. He refused to make a profit off of discoveries that could help farmers survive and feed their families. When people urged him to sell his ideas, he simply said that God had given him the knowledge and that it wasn't his to keep for himself.

Carver often spoke about kindness, humility, and faith. He didn't see himself as important, despite all the awards and recognition he had received. He called himself "just a humble servant" and focused on the work rather than the praise.

The George Washington Carver National Monument

It didn't take long for leaders to realize that his life and work needed to be remembered. Less than a year after he died, something historic happened. In 1943, the U.S. Congress approved the creation of the **George Washington Carver National Monument**, the first national monument in the United States dedicated to an African American—and the first honoring someone who wasn't a U.S. president.

This was no small decision. Up until that point, national monuments had mostly been reserved for presidents, generals, and famous battlefields. But Carver's legacy was different. He hadn't led armies or built monuments of his own. He had worked with farmers, taught students, and made discoveries that changed agriculture. He had spent his life making the world a better place, not for power or money, but because he believed it was the right thing to do.

The monument was built in **Diamond, Missouri**, the small rural town where Carver had been born into slavery. The land that had once been a farm now became a place where people could walk in the same fields where Carver first became curious about nature, where he first studied plants, and where he first dreamed of something bigger.

At the heart of the monument is a visitor center filled with exhibits about Carver's life. Visitors can learn about his childhood, his struggles to get an education, and his scientific discoveries. His personal items, including tools from his Tuskegee laboratory, letters, and photographs, are displayed to show the real man behind the legend.

But perhaps the most special part of the monument isn't inside a building—it's outside, in the very land where Carver once played as a child.

There are **trails that wind through the woods** where he once wandered, fields where he studied plants, and even a replica of the simple cabin where he was born. Along the way, signs tell stories about Carver's early years, the lessons he learned from nature, and how those lessons shaped the rest of his life.

One of the most powerful sights is a statue of Carver himself, standing tall and thoughtful, as if he's still teaching, still guiding, still encouraging people to learn and grow.

The monument became more than just a tribute.

It became a **place of learning**, just as Carver would have wanted. Every year, thousands of students visit to study his work and walk the same paths he once walked. Scientists, farmers, and historians visit to honor his contributions. Families come to hear his story and understand how one man's determination and kindness could change the world.

Carver once said, "**It is not the style of clothes one wears, neither the kind of automobile one drives, nor the amount of money one has in the bank that counts. These mean nothing. It is simply service that measures success.**"

The monument stands as proof that his success wasn't measured by wealth or status, but by how much he gave to others. His legacy is not just in the exhibits or the trails—it's in the people who continue to be inspired by his story, who learn from his discoveries, and who carry his spirit of curiosity and generosity into the future.

How his work still impacts farming and science today

How His Work Still Impacts Farming and Science Today

George Washington Carver's discoveries weren't

just useful in his time—they are still shaping the way people farm, grow food, and study science today. His ideas about agriculture, sustainability, and self-sufficiency laid the foundation for farming practices that are still used all over the world. His contributions weren't just about peanuts and sweet potatoes; they were about making sure the land could keep providing for future generations.

One of the biggest ways Carver's work lives on is through **crop rotation**. He spent years teaching farmers that planting the same crop, like cotton, over and over again would wear out the soil. It was one of the reasons so many farmers struggled to make a living—after a few years, their land stopped producing good crops. Carver's research showed that rotating crops—switching between cotton, peanuts, sweet potatoes, and other plants—would restore the soil's nutrients and keep farms productive.

Today, crop rotation isn't just a suggestion—it's standard practice. Farmers all over the world use rotation methods based on the same principles Carver taught over 100 years ago. Scientists continue to study which crops work best for soil health, and modern farming has been built around these techniques.

Carver also promoted **organic farming** long

before it became a movement. He encouraged farmers to make their own compost instead of relying on expensive chemical fertilizers. He taught them how natural materials like leaves, manure, and food scraps could enrich the soil without harming the environment. Now, as more people look for eco-friendly farming solutions, Carver's ideas about working with the land instead of against it have become even more important.

His research on **alternative crops** continues to influence agriculture. He proved that peanuts and sweet potatoes could be valuable crops for struggling farmers. Today, these crops are major industries, used for food, biofuels, and even industrial materials. The peanut industry alone is worth billions of dollars, and sweet potatoes are grown worldwide as a nutritious food source.

Beyond farming, Carver's work with **plant-based products** helped shape modern science and industry. When he discovered how to turn peanuts and sweet potatoes into paints, oils, rubber, and plastics, he was ahead of his time. Now, scientists are expanding on those ideas to create **biodegradable plastics, plant-based fuels, and eco-friendly products**. His belief that plants could be used for more than just food paved the way for today's green technology.

Even medicine has been influenced by Carver's work. He explored the healing properties of plants and natural oils, creating simple remedies for common ailments. While modern medicine has advanced far beyond his early experiments, there is a renewed interest in **plant-based medicine and natural treatments**, many of which connect back to the same ideas he studied at Tuskegee.

7

FUN FACTS ABOUT GEORGE WASHINGTON CARVER

George Washington Carver had a way with plants. He didn't just study them—he seemed to understand them. The way he worked with crops, the way he could look at soil and know what it needed, and the way he found hundreds of uses for simple plants like peanuts and sweet potatoes made some people believe he had a special connection with nature.

Over the years, a story spread that Carver talked to plants. People said he would walk through fields and gardens, speaking softly to flowers, trees, and crops as if they could hear him. Some found it odd. Others thought it was proof of his genius.

But did he really talk to plants?

The truth is, Carver **did** believe that plants had something to say—if people were willing to listen.

To him, plants weren't just things that grew from the ground. They were part of a bigger system, connected to the soil, the weather, the insects, and the people who depended on them. He often said that nature held secrets, and if you paid attention, it would reveal them.

Carver spent hours in the fields, touching leaves, feeling the texture of the soil, and observing how plants responded to light, water, and different conditions. He believed that plants communicated—not with words, but through the way they grew. A weak plant might be telling you the soil was bad. A strong plant might mean the land was healthy. A crop that wilted at the same time every day might be showing signs of too much heat or too little water.

He encouraged his students to develop the same kind of awareness. He wanted them to go beyond textbooks and learn by watching, experimenting, and connecting with the land. Science, he believed, wasn't just about working in a lab—it was about paying attention to the world.

Did he literally speak to plants? Some who knew him said he did. They recalled seeing him whisper to flowers or murmur to crops as he walked through the fields. But to Carver, this wasn't strange. To him, plants were part of God's creation, and talking to them was no different than talking to people or animals.

He often spoke about how his ideas came to him in moments of quiet reflection. He believed that the answers to his scientific questions were already in nature, waiting to be discovered. Sometimes, he would wake up early in the morning, walk outside, and feel as if the plants were guiding him toward new ideas.

The peanut and sweet potato myths

Over the years, many stories have been told about George Washington Carver, but not all of them are true. Some facts got stretched, some details got mixed up, and some people, wanting to honor his work, accidentally gave him credit for things he didn't actually do. Two of the biggest myths about Carver are that he **invented peanut butter** and that he **saved the South with peanuts and sweet potatoes.**

Carver himself never spread these myths. In fact, he often tried to correct people when they got the facts wrong. But the stories stuck anyway.

The Peanut Butter Myth

If you ask people what George Washington Carver is most famous for, many will say, "He invented peanut butter!" That's what history books, websites, and even some teachers have said for years. But the truth is, **Carver did not invent peanut butter.**

Peanut butter existed long before Carver ever started studying peanuts. Ancient civilizations, like the Aztecs and the Incas, were grinding peanuts into a paste hundreds of years ago. By the time Carver was researching peanuts, there were already patents for peanut butter in the United States. In fact, in the late 1800s, a doctor named John Harvey Kellogg (yes, the same Kellogg behind the cereal brand) had already created a version of peanut butter to help patients who had trouble chewing regular food.

Carver never claimed to have invented peanut butter. What he **did** do was find over **300** different uses for peanuts, from peanut oil to peanut-based glue. He helped farmers understand the value of peanuts as a crop. He showed people how peanuts could be used in everyday products. But peanut butter? That was not his invention.

Still, because of his strong connection to peanut research, people continued to associate him with peanut butter. The peanut industry even honored him for his contributions, even though he wasn't responsible for America's love of peanut butter sandwiches.

Did Peanuts and Sweet Potatoes Save the South?

Another common myth is that Carver **saved Southern agriculture by introducing peanuts and sweet potatoes.** While it's true that he encouraged farmers to grow these crops, he didn't exactly "introduce" them. Peanuts and sweet potatoes were already being grown in the United States long before Carver's time. What he did was **find new ways to use them and show farmers how they could restore the soil.**

During the late 1800s and early 1900s, cotton farming had drained the land of its nutrients. The soil was exhausted, and farmers were struggling. Carver knew that peanuts and sweet potatoes could help restore the land. Peanuts, like other legumes, put nitrogen back into the soil, making it healthier for future crops. Sweet potatoes were hardy and could grow in soil that was too weak for cotton.

Carver **taught farmers how to use crop rotation** —planting peanuts or sweet potatoes one season, then planting cotton the next. This method improved the soil and helped farmers grow better crops.

But the idea that peanuts and sweet potatoes single-handedly "saved the South" is an exaggeration. Agriculture is complex, and many factors played a role in improving farming in the South. Carver's teachings were incredibly important, but they were **part of a larger movement** toward better farming practices.

Why Do These Myths Exist?

People love a simple, powerful story, and Carver's life was already inspiring. He had risen from slavery to become one of the most respected scientists in the country. He had helped poor farmers and changed agriculture forever. That was already an incredible story—but some people wanted to make it even bigger.

The peanut butter myth likely started because Carver became known as "The Peanut Man." People heard about his peanut research and assumed he must have been the one who created peanut butter. The idea that he "saved the South" probably came from how much he helped farmers recover from years of poor soil conditions. Over time, the myths became more popular than the real history.

How he turned down great wealth to keep helping farmers

George Washington Carver never cared about money. That might sound surprising for someone who made so many discoveries, met powerful people, and was offered incredible opportunities. He could have been a millionaire. He could have owned a mansion, a fleet of cars, and a laboratory filled with the best equipment in the world. But none of that interested him.

He believed that science and knowledge should be used to help people, not to make a fortune. And throughout his life, he proved that belief over and over again.

A Job Offer Worth a Fortune

One of the biggest opportunities of his life came in 1920 when a letter arrived from Thomas Edison, the famous inventor behind the electric light bulb. Edison had heard about Carver's work and was impressed. He saw Carver as a brilliant scientist and problem-solver, someone who could bring new ideas to his research team.

Edison wasn't just offering a handshake and a compliment. He was offering Carver a job—a position working at Edison's lab in New Jersey. And with it came an **annual salary of $100,000.**

At the time, this was an enormous amount of money. To put it in perspective, most workers in the United States were earning less than $1,500 a year. With that salary, Carver could have lived in luxury for the rest of his life.

But he said no.

He turned down the job, the money, and everything that came with it. He had no interest in working for a company, no matter how famous it was. His heart was in Tuskegee, with his students and the farmers who needed his help.

Carver knew that if he worked for Edison, he'd be making discoveries that would help a business, not struggling farmers. And to him, that wasn't what science was for.

Refusing to Patent His Discoveries

Turning down Edison's offer wasn't the only time Carver refused to make money from his work. He developed **over 300 uses for peanuts** and **over 100 uses for sweet potatoes**, but he never patented most of them.

Companies wanted to buy his formulas, put his name on products, and pay him for his discoveries. But he refused.

When people asked why he didn't want to make a fortune, he had a simple answer:

"God gave them to me; how can I sell them to someone else?"

Carver believed that knowledge was a gift, something to be shared freely. He wanted farmers to benefit from his discoveries, not businessmen. If a poor farmer could make peanut oil at home instead of buying expensive oil from a store, that was more important to him than a patent.

He did patent a few inventions, including a peanut-based skin lotion and a type of paint, but even those he refused to make a profit from. He said he only patented them to prevent companies from taking the credit.

Living a Simple Life

Even as he became famous, Carver never changed the way he lived. He still woke up before dawn, still worked long hours in his lab, and still ate simple meals—often just milk and boiled peanuts.

He never owned a car. If he needed to go somewhere, he walked or accepted rides from friends. He wore the same old suit for years, patching it up when it started to wear out. He didn't spend money on fancy furniture, expensive meals, or anything flashy.

Some people couldn't understand it. They

thought he was strange for refusing to take money for his work. They thought he should accept wealth as a reward for all he had done. But Carver didn't see it that way.

To him, success wasn't about what you owned. It was about what you gave to others.

A Gift to Tuskegee

As he got older, Carver still had no interest in money for himself, but he did think about how he could continue helping others after he was gone. Instead of keeping what little money he had, he donated it.

He established the **George Washington Carver Foundation**, which provided funding for agricultural research at Tuskegee. He wanted future scientists to have the resources to keep improving farming, to keep discovering, and to keep making life better for people.

His advice for young scientists and dreamers

George Washington Carver never believed that science was only for people in fancy laboratories or those with expensive equipment. He knew that curiosity, determination, and kindness mattered more than wealth or status. Throughout his life, he shared wisdom with students, farmers, and anyone willing to listen. His advice still resonates today for young scientists, inventors, and dreamers.

Start with What You Have

Carver grew up with almost nothing. He was born into slavery, had no formal school for much of his childhood, and had to walk miles just to get an education. When he became a scientist, his laboratory at Tuskegee was small, and he didn't have high-tech tools. But he never let that stop him.

He made do with what was available. If he didn't have the right test tubes, he used bottles. If he needed equipment, he built it himself. When his students complained about not having enough materials, he reminded them that science isn't about expensive tools—it's about curiosity and problem-solving.

Carver's lesson was clear: **Don't wait for perfect conditions to start learning and creating. Use what you have and make the most of it.**

Ask Questions, and Then Find the Answers

Carver believed that every great discovery started with a simple question. As a child, he asked why plants grew the way they did, why soil became weak, and how nature worked together. Those questions led him to experiment, observe, and learn.

He encouraged his students to be curious, to never accept things at face value, and to test their ideas. When someone told him something couldn't be done, he didn't argue—he experimented. He let science provide the answer.

For anyone wanting to be a scientist, inventor, or problem solver, his advice was simple: **Stay curious. Keep asking "why?" and "how?" And don't just accept what people say—test it for yourself.**

Work Hard, but with Purpose

Carver worked tirelessly, waking up before dawn and spending long hours in his lab. But he wasn't working for money or fame. He was working to **help others.**

He believed that talent and intelligence weren't enough—what mattered was how you used them. He often told his students that success wasn't about personal gain but about what you could give back to the world.

Hard work is important, but **working with purpose** is even more powerful. Carver's advice? **Use your talents to make life better for others. That's the true measure of success.**

Be Patient, and Keep Going

Science takes time. Many of Carver's discoveries didn't happen overnight. He spent years studying soil, plants, and crop rotation before farmers finally listened. He experimented with peanuts and sweet potatoes for years before he found hundreds of uses for them.

He knew that not every experiment would work the first time. He knew that some people would doubt him. But he also knew that perseverance—sticking with something even when it's hard—was the key to making real progress.

His advice to young dreamers? **Don't give up when things don't work right away. Keep learning, keep trying, and trust that persistence leads to success.**

Stay Humble, Stay Kind

Even though Carver became famous, met presidents, and was offered enormous wealth, he remained humble. He never bragged about his achievements. He never looked down on others. Instead, he saw himself as a servant—someone who was there to teach, to help, and to make the world better.

He treated everyone with kindness, no matter who they were. He never spoke harshly, even to those who doubted him. He believed that the best way to change the world was **not through anger or pride, but through patience and kindness.**

For young scientists and dreamers, this is perhaps his greatest lesson: **Be kind. Stay humble. Let your work speak for itself.**

Leave the World Better Than You Found It

Carver didn't just want to make discoveries—he wanted to make a difference. That's why he never sought wealth from his inventions. That's why he dedicated his life to teaching and helping farmers. He believed that every person had a responsibility to make the world better in some way.

His words still hold power today:

"**It is not the style of clothes one wears, neither the kind of automobile one drives, nor the amount of money one has in the bank that counts. These mean nothing. It is simply service that measures success.**"

For anyone with big dreams, his message is clear: **Use your talents to help others. Share your knowledge. Make a difference. That's what truly matters.**

CONCLUSION: WHAT WE CAN LEARN FROM CARVER

George Washington Carver believed that **learning was the key to everything**. He had spent his whole life chasing knowledge, even when it seemed impossible to get an education. He understood that **education wasn't just about school—it was about asking questions, discovering answers, and always wanting to know more.** To him, curiosity and education went hand in hand.

Curiosity: The First Step to Learning

Carver never waited for someone to tell him what to study. As a child, he explored the world around him, fascinated by the plants, soil, and animals he found on the farm. He wanted to know how things worked—why flowers bloomed, why dirt changed color, why crops failed in bad soil but thrived in good soil.

When he was young, he didn't have books or a teacher to answer these questions. **But that didn't stop him.** He learned by observing, experimenting, and testing ideas on his own. If one idea didn't work, he tried another. If he couldn't find an answer, he searched until he did.

His curiosity didn't fade as he grew older. Even after he became a scientist, he never stopped asking questions. He was always looking for new ways to help farmers, new ways to improve crops, and new ways to use plants in everyday life.

Curiosity, he believed, was **the secret to discovery.** Whether it was a young child wondering how a peanut could be turned into paint, or a scientist looking for a way to make farming better, everything started with a question.

Education: A Lifelong Journey

Carver knew that **education was more than just memorizing facts—it was about understanding the world.** He believed that learning should never stop, no matter how old you were.

He had to fight for his education. There were no schools for Black children where he lived, so he left home and walked miles to find one. When he wanted more, he traveled even farther, working hard to support himself while he studied. There were people who told him he would never succeed. There were times when it seemed impossible. But he refused to give up.

He didn't just want education for himself—he wanted to share it. At Tuskegee Institute, he became more than a teacher; he became a mentor. He encouraged students to think for themselves, to question everything, and to **use their education to improve the lives of others.**

For Carver, education wasn't about passing tests or getting degrees. **It was about using knowledge to make a difference.**

The Power of Asking "Why?"

One of Carver's favorite sayings was, **"Start where you are, with what you have. Make something of it. Never be satisfied."**

He wanted people to **ask why**—why things worked the way they did, why problems happened, and how they could be solved.

Many of his greatest discoveries came from asking simple questions. Why was the soil in the South so bad? Why did peanuts grow better than cotton? Could sweet potatoes be turned into useful products? Each question led him to a new answer, a new discovery, and a new way to help farmers and families.

Learning Beyond the Classroom

Carver understood that **education isn't just something that happens in school.** It happens everywhere—in nature, in experiments, in failures, and in everyday life.

He learned just as much from plants, farmers, and soil as he did from books. That's why he encouraged students to **get their hands dirty**, to learn by doing, and to never be afraid of failure.

He also believed that education wasn't just about science or farming—it was about developing character, treating people with kindness, and making the world better.

A Message for Future Learners

Carver's life was proof that **curiosity and education can open doors, change lives, and create endless possibilities.**

He didn't come from a rich family. He didn't have special advantages. But **he had a love of learning, and that was enough.**

His message to young scientists, inventors, and dreamers was simple:

- **Be curious.** Ask questions. Never stop wondering how things work.
- **Seek knowledge.** Learn wherever you can, from books, from nature, from people around you.
- **Work hard.** Education takes effort, but it is always worth it.
- **Use your knowledge for good.** The best education is the kind that helps others.

Carver proved that **education isn't about where you come from—it's about where you're willing to go.** And as long as curiosity leads the way, there are no limits.

Helping others with knowledge

His entire life was proof of this belief. Every time he made a discovery, he didn't try to keep it secret or sell it to the highest bidder. He gave his knowledge away freely, making sure it reached the people who needed it most.

Teaching Farmers, Not Just Students

At Tuskegee Institute, Carver's students weren't the only ones learning from him. He realized that many farmers—especially Black farmers in the

South—had never been taught how to improve their land. They had been growing cotton the same way for generations, even though their soil was weak and their crops were failing.

Carver knew that if he wanted to help people, he couldn't just teach students in a classroom. He needed to take his knowledge directly to the farmers.

He and his students loaded up a **Jesup Wagon,** a movable classroom filled with seeds, farming tools, and soil samples, and traveled from town to town. They showed farmers how to rotate crops to keep their soil healthy, how to grow peanuts and sweet potatoes to rebuild the land, and how to make products from their crops instead of relying only on selling raw cotton.

Many of these farmers had no money for expensive fertilizers, so Carver taught them how to make compost from natural materials. Instead of buying soap, they learned how to make their own. Instead of throwing away peanut shells, they learned how to turn them into useful products.

His goal wasn't just to teach farming—it was to teach **self-sufficiency.** He wanted farmers to know that **they had the power to improve their lives, even if they didn't have much to start with.**

Encouraging Future Scientists

Carver didn't stop at helping farmers. He wanted the next generation to know that science wasn't just something done in big laboratories—it was something they could do, too.

He encouraged his students to ask questions, experiment, and use their knowledge to help others. He challenged them to **think beyond what they were taught** and come up with new ideas. He reminded them that no discovery was too small if it could improve someone's life.

Many of his students went on to become teachers, scientists, and leaders in their communities. Carver's influence didn't just stop with the people he directly taught—it spread through his students, reaching even more people across the country.

Sharing Ideas Freely

One of the most remarkable things about Carver was his refusal to profit from his discoveries. Many scientists try to **patent** their inventions, which means no one else can use them without permission or payment. Carver didn't believe in that.

When people asked why he didn't try to make money from his peanut discoveries, he answered, **"God gave them to me; how can I sell them?"**

To him, science was meant to **serve people, not to make one person rich.** He believed that his knowledge should be available to everyone, not just those who could afford it.

Because of this, he freely shared his research with anyone who wanted to learn. Farmers, teachers, students, and business owners all benefited from his discoveries. His ideas were published in pamphlets, given out at no cost, and spread through his travels and lectures.

Helping on a Larger Scale

Carver's reputation for helping others spread beyond the fields and classrooms. People in high places—presidents, business leaders, and even world-famous inventors—sought his advice. He met with Theodore Roosevelt, Henry Ford, and even Mahatma Gandhi, who admired Carver's self-sufficient farming methods and wanted to use them in India.

Despite meeting powerful people, Carver always remained the same humble teacher. He never let fame change his mission. Whether he was speaking to a president or a struggling farmer, his message was the same: **knowledge is power, but only if you share it.**

Taking care of the land

He had seen what happened when farmers **took from the soil without giving anything back.** They planted cotton, season after season, pulling all the nutrients out of the earth. Over time, their fields stopped producing strong crops. The land was exhausted. The farmers struggled, their families suffered, and entire communities faced hardship.

Carver believed that nature and farming should work together, not against each other. He spent his life **teaching people how to take care of the land so it could keep providing for generations to come.**

Listening to the Soil

Carver didn't just look at plants—he studied the soil itself. He believed that **healthy soil meant healthy crops,** and unhealthy soil led to failure. While some farmers focused only on what was growing above the ground, Carver paid attention to what was beneath it.

He taught that soil wasn't just dirt—it was a **living thing** filled with nutrients. Just like people needed food to stay strong, the soil needed certain elements to stay fertile. He showed farmers how different plants took different nutrients from the ground, and how some plants, like peanuts and sweet potatoes, actually gave nutrients back.

To help farmers see this in action, he often **dug into the dirt with his own hands**, feeling its texture, smelling it, and examining its color. If the soil was dry and crumbly, it needed more moisture. If it was pale, it lacked nutrients. If plants were growing weakly, something in the soil was off. He encouraged farmers to do the same—**to pay attention to what the land was telling them.**

Rotating Crops to Keep the Land Strong

One of Carver's biggest lessons was the **importance of crop rotation.** Instead of growing cotton year after year, he encouraged farmers to switch crops each season.

Cotton was **hard on the land.** It stripped the soil of nitrogen, an important nutrient for plant growth. But peanuts, peas, and sweet potatoes actually **put nitrogen back into the soil.** Carver explained that if farmers planted these crops in between cotton seasons, they could restore their land naturally.

Many farmers were skeptical at first. They had grown cotton their entire lives—why change now? But those who followed Carver's advice **began to see their land improve.** Their crops were healthier, their soil held moisture better, and their farms became more productive.

Carver didn't just tell people to rotate crops—he **showed them**. He would plant peanuts in poor soil, then return a year later and plant cotton in the same spot. The cotton that grew after peanuts was noticeably stronger. Seeing the results for themselves, more and more farmers began adopting his methods.

Using Every Resource Wisely

Carver believed that nothing should go to waste. If a plant or a material had a use, he would find it.

Many farmers only thought of peanuts and sweet potatoes as food, but Carver discovered **hundreds of ways** to use them. He made **paints, oils, soaps, rubber, glue, and even ink** from these plants, proving that they were more valuable than people realized.

His ability to see new possibilities in everyday things was part of his genius. Instead of throwing out peanut shells, he found ways to use them in animal feed. Instead of burning corn husks, he found ways to turn them into paper. Instead of relying on store-bought fertilizer, he encouraged farmers to **make their own compost from food scraps and plant waste**.

For Carver, **nature already provided everything people needed—they just had to learn how to use it wisely.**

Respecting the Land

Carver didn't see nature as something to be controlled—he saw it as something to be respected. He believed that people should **work with the land, not against it.**

When other scientists focused on factory-made chemicals to fix soil problems, Carver looked for **natural solutions.** He wanted to find ways to farm that were sustainable, meaning they could continue for generations without destroying the land.

His ideas were far ahead of his time. Today, farmers and scientists still use his principles to practice **sustainable agriculture,** making sure the land stays healthy for the future. His teachings on **crop rotation, composting, and using natural resources** are still essential in modern farming.

GLOSSARY
AGRICULTURE

Agriculture is **the science and practice of growing plants and raising animals for food, materials, and other useful products.** It's one of the oldest things people have done. Thousands of years ago, humans figured out that instead of moving from place to place searching for food, they could plant seeds, grow crops, and raise animals in one place.

Without agriculture, people wouldn't have fresh vegetables, fruits, grains, or dairy. It's what makes grocery stores full of food and what keeps the world fed. But agriculture is more than just growing food—it also includes raising animals for milk, meat, and wool, as well as growing plants for materials like cotton or rubber.

Carver wanted farmers to **think about agricul-**

ture as a way to work with nature, not just take from it. He taught them how to keep their land healthy so it could provide food for generations.

Crop Rotation

Crop rotation is **the practice of planting different types of crops in the same field at different times to keep the soil healthy.** Instead of growing the same thing over and over, farmers switch crops each season to prevent the land from wearing out.

Some crops, like cotton, **take a lot of nutrients from the soil,** leaving it weak and unhealthy. Others, like peanuts and peas, **put nutrients back into the soil,** making it stronger. Carver taught farmers that by rotating their crops, they could protect their land and **grow better, healthier food.**

For example:

- Year 1: A farmer plants cotton.
- Year 2: The farmer plants peanuts, which return nitrogen to the soil.
- Year 3: The farmer plants corn, which benefits from the richer soil.
- Year 4: The farmer plants sweet potatoes, another crop that improves soil quality.

Glossary

By doing this, the soil stays **rich and balanced**, allowing the farm to produce more food over time.

Soil Depletion

Soil depletion happens when the land **loses its nutrients because the same crops are planted over and over without giving the soil a chance to recover.**

This was a huge problem during Carver's time. Many farmers in the South planted **only cotton** because it sold for good money. But cotton took important nutrients from the soil, and after many years, the land became dry and weak. The plants grew smaller, the fields produced less, and farmers struggled to survive.

Carver showed farmers that **soil needed care, just like a plant or an animal.** He encouraged them to plant peanuts, sweet potatoes, and other crops that would **return nutrients to the land.** This helped stop soil depletion and made farming more successful.

Compost

Compost is **a natural way to make soil healthier.** It's made from food scraps, leaves, grass clippings, and other organic materials that break down over time. Instead of throwing away fruit peels, vegetable scraps, or yard waste, farmers (and even people with home gardens) can **turn them into rich soil full of nutrients.**

Carver encouraged farmers to use compost instead of expensive store-bought fertilizers. It was a simple way to **feed the soil naturally** while reducing waste.

Sustainable Farming

Sustainable farming means **growing food in a way that protects the land, water, and air, so future generations can keep farming.** It's about using nature wisely and **not taking more than the land can give.**

Carver was ahead of his time when it came to sustainability. He encouraged farmers to **rotate crops, build compost, and find new uses for plants.** His ideas helped protect the environment long before people started using words like "sustainability."

Legumes

Legumes are a special type of plant that **help fix soil by adding nitrogen back into it.** Some of the most common legumes include:

- **Peanuts**
- **Peas**
- **Beans**

- Clover

Carver loved legumes because they **did two things at once**—they gave farmers a crop they could eat or sell while also **restoring the health of the soil**.

Mulch

Mulch is **a layer of plant material, like straw, leaves, or wood chips, that is spread over soil to protect it**. It helps keep the soil **moist, cool, and full of nutrients**.

Carver encouraged farmers to use mulch because it reduced the need for watering and prevented weeds from growing. This made farming easier and saved resources.

Organic Farming

Organic farming means **growing food without using artificial chemicals, like pesticides and synthetic fertilizers**. Instead, it relies on natural methods like compost, crop rotation, and healthy soil to grow strong plants.

Carver believed that nature had **everything people needed to farm successfully**. He encouraged using plants, minerals, and organic waste instead of harmful chemicals. Today, organic farming is widely used because it **protects the environment and produces healthier food.**

Self-Sufficiency

Carver often spoke about self-sufficiency, which means **being able to take care of yourself and your community without always depending on outside help.** He wanted farmers to know how to make their own products, grow their own food, and use their land wisely.

Instead of buying expensive products from stores, Carver taught people how to:

- Make their own **fertilizer** from compost
- Create **dyes and paints** from sweet potatoes and peanuts
- Produce **homemade soap, oils, and cleaning products**

He believed that **knowledge was the key to independence.** The more people knew, the more they could do for themselves.

DISCUSSION QUESTIONS
WHAT WOULD YOU DO IN HIS SHOES?

Carver was born into slavery, but he didn't let his circumstances stop him from pursuing knowledge. He walked miles just to attend school and worked hard to keep learning, even when others told him he couldn't.

- **Have you ever faced a challenge where someone told you that you couldn't do something? How did you respond?**
- **If you were in Carver's position, do you think you would have had the same determination to keep learning? Why or why not?**
- **What would you have done if you had to walk miles just to go to school?**

Would you keep going, or would you find another way to learn?

Curiosity and Asking Questions

Carver's success came from his **endless curiosity**. He didn't just accept the way things were—he asked why. Why did the soil become weak? Why did some plants grow better than others? Why couldn't farmers make more money from their crops? His constant questioning led to discoveries that changed agriculture forever.

- What is something you've always been curious about?
- Have you ever asked a question that led to you discovering something new? What happened?
- How do you think the world would be different if people stopped asking questions?
- If Carver were alive today, what scientific problems do you think he would try to solve?

Helping Others with Knowledge

Carver believed that knowledge should be

shared freely. He never tried to make a fortune from his discoveries. Instead, he gave his ideas away so farmers, students, and communities could benefit.

- If you discovered something amazing, would you share it with the world or keep it to yourself? Why?
- Why do you think Carver refused to get rich from his inventions?
- Do you think helping others is more important than making money? Why or why not?
- Can you think of ways you could use what you know to help someone else?

Using Resources Wisely

Carver believed in **working with nature instead of against it.** He taught farmers to rotate crops, compost waste, and find new uses for plants so nothing went to waste.

- Why is it important to take care of the land and the environment?
- Can you think of ways people waste natural resources today?

- What is something small you could do to take better care of nature?
- If you had to invent something that helped the environment, what would it be?

The Power of Perseverance

Carver faced many obstacles—poverty, racism, rejection from schools—but he **never gave up**. He kept learning, kept experimenting, and kept pushing forward no matter what.

- Have you ever worked really hard for something, even when it was difficult? How did it feel?
- What do you think kept Carver from giving up, even when life was hard?
- If you were struggling with a problem, what advice do you think Carver would give you?
- Why is it important to keep trying even when things don't go the way you planned?

Science as a Tool for Change

Carver didn't just do science for fun—he used it

to **help others.** His discoveries in farming, soil health, and plant-based products made life better for thousands of people.

- Do you think science can change the world? How?
- What problem would you want to solve using science?
- Carver didn't have fancy tools when he started experimenting. What are some ways you could explore science using what you have around you?
- If Carver could see today's world, what do you think he would say about it?

Thinking About the Future

Carver didn't just think about his own success—he thought about how his work would help **future generations.** He wanted people to farm smarter, use resources wisely, and **continue learning long after he was gone.**

- What lessons from Carver's life do you think are still important today?
- If you could talk to Carver, what question would you ask him?

- **What is one thing you can learn from his story that you could use in your own life?**
- **Do you think Carver would be happy with the way people treat the environment today? Why or why not?**

Carver believed that education, curiosity, and kindness were the keys to making the world better. His story isn't just about the past—it's about what's possible when someone **keeps learning, keeps questioning, and keeps helping others.** The real question now is:

What will you do with what you've learned?

SIMPLE SCIENCE ACTIVITIES

Here are some simple activities that let you **experiment with farming and plants** just like Carver did. You don't need fancy tools or expensive supplies. Just curiosity and a willingness to try.

1. Does Soil Affect Plant Growth?

Carver spent a lot of time studying **soil health**. He wanted farmers to know that if the soil wasn't healthy, their crops wouldn't grow well. This experiment will show how different soils affect plant growth.

What You'll Need:

- Three small containers (cups, pots, or yogurt cups)

- Three types of soil (garden soil, sand, and clay)
- Water
- Seeds (beans, peas, or sunflower seeds work well)

Steps:

1. Fill each container with a different type of soil.
2. Plant one seed in each container, making sure to bury it about an inch deep.
3. Water all three containers the same amount every day.
4. Place them in a sunny spot.
5. Keep a journal and write down what happens each day.

What to Look For:

- Which soil helps the plant grow best?
- Does one type of soil dry out faster?
- Do the plants in certain soils grow taller or healthier than others?

This is the same type of experiment Carver did

when he studied soil **to help farmers grow better crops.**

2. The Power of Crop Rotation

Carver taught farmers to **rotate crops** to keep the soil strong. You can test this idea using something as simple as a jar of water.

What You'll Need:

- Two clear jars of water
- One teaspoon of sugar
- One teaspoon of baking soda
- A spoon for stirring

Steps:

1. In one jar, add sugar and stir until it dissolves.
2. Keep adding sugar, one teaspoon at a time, and stir after each addition.
3. In the second jar, add sugar first, then switch to adding baking soda after a few teaspoons.

What to Look For:

- In the first jar, the water eventually won't dissolve any more sugar—just like soil running out of nutrients.
- In the second jar, switching ingredients (like switching crops) **helps balance the mixture.**

Carver used crop rotation in the same way—**switching crops kept the soil from wearing out.**

3. Grow a Peanut or Sweet Potato Vine

Carver found **hundreds of uses** for peanuts and sweet potatoes. You can grow your own at home and watch how plants develop.

What You'll Need:

- A raw peanut in its shell OR a sweet potato
- A small glass jar or plastic cup
- Toothpicks
- Water

Steps (for a Peanut Plant):

1. Remove the shell from a raw peanut.
2. Wrap the peanut in a damp paper towel and place it inside a plastic bag.

3. Check daily to see when it sprouts, then plant it in a pot with soil.

Steps (for a Sweet Potato Vine):

1. Stick 3-4 toothpicks into the middle of a sweet potato, about halfway up the sides.
2. Place the sweet potato in a jar so that the bottom half is in the water and the top half stays dry.
3. Put it in a sunny spot and change the water every few days.
4. Watch as roots and vines grow from the sweet potato.

Carver grew these crops not just for food but for **soil health and making useful products.**

4. Can Plants Tell the Time? (Phototropism Experiment)

Carver spent a lot of time **observing how plants responded to their environment.** One thing he noticed was how plants grow toward sunlight. You can test this for yourself.

What You'll Need:

- A cardboard box

- A small plant in a cup or pot
- Scissors

Steps:

1. Cut a small hole in one side of the box.
2. Place the plant inside the box, making sure the hole lets in some sunlight.
3. Check the plant each day to see if it starts **bending toward the light.**

What's Happening?

Plants grow toward sunlight because they need it to make food. This process is called **phototropism.** Carver studied how plants reacted to different conditions to help farmers understand **how to grow stronger crops.**

5. Make Natural Plant Dye Like Carver Did

Carver didn't just grow plants for food—he found ways to make **paints and dyes from them.** You can create your own natural dye from fruits and vegetables.

What You'll Need:

- Fruits or vegetables (beets, blueberries,

spinach, onion skins, or turmeric work well)
- A small pot
- Water
- A white cloth or paper

Steps:

1. Chop up the fruits or vegetables and place them in a pot.
2. Add water until the plant materials are covered.
3. Simmer for about 30 minutes.
4. Strain out the solid pieces, leaving just the colored liquid.
5. Dip a cloth or paper into the dye and see how the color sticks.

Carver experimented with **natural dyes** to create alternatives to chemical-based paints.

6. Test the Power of Compost

Instead of throwing away food scraps, Carver encouraged farmers to **use compost to feed the soil.** You can create a simple compost experiment at home.

What You'll Need:

- Two clear plastic containers
- Soil
- Food scraps (banana peel, apple core, lettuce)
- A plastic spoon

Steps:

1. Fill both containers with soil.
2. In one container, mix in food scraps and stir with the spoon. Leave the other container plain.
3. Keep both containers in the same spot and water them lightly every few days.
4. After two weeks, compare the two containers.

What to Look For:

- The container with food scraps should be darker and **richer in nutrients.**
- The other container may start to look dry or depleted.

Carver taught that compost **keeps soil healthy without needing chemical fertilizers.**

CAREERS IN SCIENCE AND AGRICULTURE

George Washington Carver didn't just love learning about plants and farming—he turned that passion into a lifetime of discovery, teaching, and helping others. He believed that science wasn't just something you learned in school; it was something you could use to **solve real-world problems and make life better for people.**

Today, there are **many careers** that focus on science, agriculture, and the environment. Whether someone loves plants, animals, technology, or research, there's a way to **turn curiosity into a future job.**

Carver would have encouraged students to **start exploring early.** He believed that anyone, no matter where they came from, could **ask questions, experi-**

ment, and turn what they loved into something meaningful.

Plant Scientists: Helping Crops Grow Stronger

Carver spent years studying soil and plants to figure out how to improve farming. Today, **plant scientists (also called agronomists or botanists)** do the same thing!

What they do:

- Study how different plants grow in different environments.
- Find ways to make crops healthier and more resistant to disease.
- Discover new plants that can be used for food, medicine, or materials.

Ways to explore:

- **Grow different types of plants** in your backyard or in containers.
- **Visit a botanical garden** and learn about different species.
- **Experiment with plant growth**—what happens if you change how much sunlight or water they get?

- **Learn about famous plant scientists,** including Carver, Luther Burbank, and Gregor Mendel.

Soil Scientists: Protecting the Land

Carver's research on soil health helped farmers keep their land fertile. Today, **soil scientists** study how soil affects crops, climate, and the environment.

What they do:

- Test soil for nutrients and teach farmers how to improve it.
- Study erosion and help protect farmland from damage.
- Work with engineers to build better irrigation systems.

Ways to explore:

- **Collect soil samples** from different places and compare them.
- **Test how different materials (sand, clay, compost) affect plant growth.**
- **Learn about erosion** by watching what happens when water flows over bare soil.

Environmental Scientists: Solving Big Problems

Carver didn't just think about farming—he cared about protecting nature. **Environmental scientists** study how humans impact the earth and find ways to fix problems like pollution and climate change.

What they do:

- Study air and water quality.
- Protect wildlife and natural resources.
- Help make farming and factories less harmful to the environment.

Ways to explore:

- **Visit a nature center** and learn about conservation.
- **Do a water quality test** on a local stream or pond.
- **Reduce waste** by learning how to compost and recycle.

Food Scientists: Making Food Better and Safer

Carver created **hundreds of uses for peanuts and sweet potatoes.** Today, **food scientists** develop new foods, make food last longer, and find healthier ways to produce meals.

What they do:

- Create new flavors and healthier versions of food.
- Study nutrition and how different foods affect the body.
- Test ways to keep food fresh without chemicals.

Ways to explore:

- **Experiment with cooking**—what happens when you mix different ingredients?
- **Read food labels** and learn how food is made.
- **Try growing your own food** and see how fresh ingredients taste compared to store-bought ones.

Agricultural Engineers: Inventing New Farming Tools

Carver used science to help farmers work more efficiently. Today, **agricultural engineers** design tractors, irrigation systems, and machines that make farming easier.

What they do:

- Build machines that plant and harvest crops faster.
- Design irrigation systems that use less water.
- Invent new ways to store food and keep it fresh.

Ways to explore:

- **Take apart and study machines,** like lawnmowers or bicycles, to see how they work.
- **Build simple tools** for gardening or watering plants.
- **Visit a farm** to see how modern machines help farmers.

Veterinarians and Animal Scientists: Caring for Farm Animals

Carver's work helped **not just plants, but also animals.** Veterinarians and animal scientists study **how to keep farm animals healthy** and improve farming practices for dairy, eggs, and meat.

What they do:

- Treat sick farm animals like cows, chickens, and pigs.
- Study animal behavior and nutrition.
- Help farmers raise animals in healthier ways.

Ways to explore:

- **Visit a farm or petting zoo** and observe how animals behave.
- **Learn about different breeds of farm animals** and what makes them unique.
- **Help take care of pets or volunteer at an animal shelter.**

Beekeepers and Pollination Experts: Helping Crops Grow

Carver understood that **plants depend on bees and other pollinators.** Beekeepers and pollination scientists work to protect bees and help farmers grow more crops.

What they do:

- Raise honeybees and collect honey.
- Study how pollination affects crops.
- Help farmers protect bees from pesticides.

Ways to explore:

- **Plant flowers that attract bees** and observe them in action.
- **Visit a beekeeper** and learn how honey is made.
- **Learn about the importance of pollinators** like butterflies and hummingbirds.

Urban Farmers and Hydroponics Experts: Growing Food in New Ways

Carver focused on **teaching farmers how to grow crops in tough conditions**. Today, urban farmers and hydroponics experts grow food in cities and even indoors without soil!

What they do:

- Grow vegetables on rooftops and in greenhouses.

- Use hydroponics (growing plants in water instead of soil) to grow food anywhere.
- Help communities grow their own food in small spaces.

Ways to explore:

- **Grow a small herb garden inside your home.**
- **Visit a community garden** and see how food is grown in cities.
- **Learn about vertical farming,** where crops grow on shelves instead of fields.